WITHDRAWN
UTSA LIBRARIES

RENEWALS 458-4574

THE EDGE OF MARRIAGE

Winner of the

Flannery O'Connor Award for Short Fiction

Hester Kaplan

THE EDGE OF MARRIAGE

The University of Georgia Press
Athens and London

Published by the University of Georgia Press
Athens, Georgia 30602
© 1999 by Hester Kaplan
All rights reserved
Designed by Betty Palmer McDaniel
Set in 10 on 13 Sabon by G & S Typesetters, Inc.
Printed and bound by Maple-Vail Book Group, Inc.
The paper in this book meets the guidelines for
permanence and durability of the Committee on
Production Guidelines for Book Longevity of the
Council on Library Resources.

Printed in the United States of America

03 02 01 00 99   C   5 4 3 2

Library of Congress Cataloging-in-Publication Data
Kaplan, Hester, 1959–
The edge of marriage : stories / by Hester Kaplan.
p. cm.
"Winner of the Flannery O'Connor Award for Short Fiction."
Contents: Would you know it wasn't love? —
Dysaesthesia — From where we've fallen —
Cuckle me — The edge of marriage — Goodwill —
Claude comes and goes — The spiral — Live life king-sized.
ISBN 0-8203-2148-6 (alk. paper)
1. United States—Social life and customs—20th
century—Fiction. 2. Man-woman relationships—
United States—Fiction. I. Title.
PS3561.A5577E33 1999
813'.54—dc21   99-19713

British Library Cataloging-in-Publication Data available

Library
University of Texas
at San Antonio

For Michael

ACKNOWLEDGMENTS

The stories in this collection first appeared in the following publications: "Would You Know It Wasn't Love?" in *Gulf Coast;* "Dysaesthesia" and "Live Life King-Sized" in *Press;* "From Where We've Fallen," "Cuckle Me," and "The Edge of Marriage" in *Story;* "Goodwill" in *Ploughshares;* "Claude Comes and Goes" in *Agni;* and "The Spiral" in *Glimmer Train.*

Grateful acknowledgment is made to members of the Providence Area Writers Group and to the Rhode Island State Council on the Arts. I would especially like to thank Lois Rosenthal of *Story* for her support and encouragement, Tobias and Alexander for everything, and Michael, who inspires me.

CONTENTS

THE EDGE OF MARRIAGE

WOULD YOU KNOW IT WASN'T LOVE?

When Walt thinks about his daughter Rosie and her disintegrating marriage, he can't help thinking about himself too. He's not moved to pity, either for his own sick self or for Rosie and Tim; what he feels instead is the misery and waste of this breaking-up of lives. He's edgy now when he's always been patient, but he's a man with a disease, out of control sometimes, sometimes hateful, he knows, but forgiven. His wife Helen, well ahead of him into Rosie's mess already, has bags under her eyes and a penchant for salty things which she eats until her mouth swells up. After dinner, Walt caught her gulping glass after glass of water at the kitchen sink. He felt as though he'd walked in on something he shouldn't have seen, but he couldn't look away. Recently Helen has stopped acknowledging his private moments—the time his swollen fingers refused to hold a glass, so that it fell and shattered on the floor, when his morning stiffness had him groping at the wall for something to lean against. He knows she's witnessed them. He's seen her worried shadow pass by, heard her gasp.

On the downstairs extension in his study off the kitchen, and Helen upstairs on the bedroom phone, he talks to Rosie. Walt wants to understand what's going on, but she sniffles more than she speaks a full sentence so that, again, he isn't sure what the problem is. After Rosie says good-bye to her parents, Walt and Helen stay on the line. Tim *is* brooding and inscrutable, Walt says to Helen—has she ever met a man who wasn't?—but does that mean Rosie should walk away from her marriage? It's an old theme he's brought up: the fear that they've babied their youngest daughter to the point of hobbling her.

Walt thinks it's strange—but also a little easier—to talk to Helen tonight over the phone so they don't have to look at each other. He can imagine that she's not quite as familiar to him, nor he so familiar to her, that they might come up with something they haven't said before.

The operator interrupts before Helen can answer, so Walt walks upstairs to finish the conversation. Helen turns to him as he enters the bedroom, and in the light of her reading lamp he sees the chapping around her thin mouth, like cheap lipstick. He wonders, too tired for passion, how long it has been since they've really kissed, tongues and all, with his hands on her solid body; certainly not since the start of Rosie's crisis.

"Why are you telling me this about Tim?" Helen asks him angrily, and her face blushes red. Her eyes are a cold blue. "Inscrutable? Brooding? Those are ridiculous words. What am I supposed to do with them? Are they going to help the situation somehow?"

Walt has no answer for his wife. He hadn't intended to sound so coldhearted, only firm.

Helen returns to the student papers she's correcting for tomorrow, and Walt goes downstairs to his study again. When he kneels slowly in front of the closet, he almost expects to find that the rheumatoid arthritis has reached his knees, as his doctor has warned it might one of these days. But he is relieved to be spared so far and digs around in the back where he keeps all his cassette tapes: of his lectures, the babies' chatter, of his girls' clumsy and beautiful recitals and plays, of school speeches and dinner parties, Helen's singing tipsy at his forty-seventh birthday party. He's sentimental about these sounds the way others are about photographs.

The sharp plastic boxes are a comfort to him. Walt is aware that he's a technological oddity these days, preferring his inoffensive, nonobtrusive tape recorder and cassettes when he could get sound *and* picture with a camcorder the size of his palm, the minor heft of a small melon. One day he intends to do something with all of the tapes he's collected, turn them into a kind of family history he might listen to when he's finally crippled. Through old corduroy pants, Walt's bones begin to grind against the floor, and it takes him a while to locate the cassette he's after. He finds it near the back finally, and stands up.

Walt pushes the play button on his recorder, sits in his armchair the cat has scratched bare, and listens. His study needs repainting, he sees. The bad light plays up how much they've let slide in the past two years since he's been sick, as though the only thing to focus on is the mysterious course his body is taking. He remembers four years earlier deciding to leave the tape running even as his favorite dog vomited under the kitchen table, as Helen dropped an empty pan on the floor and the dishwasher started with its splash of water. It was the noise behind the negotiations he'd wanted to record as much as the discussion itself of the wedding's guest list and the meaning of an open bar. Helen and Rosie had hardly protested against the taping and what their own words might hold them to later on, and then only because they understood it was expected of them, just as the taping was expected of him.

But Walt hears now, very clearly with nothing to distract him in his quiet house, that Tim was not so sure about being recorded, collected. The boy clears his throat too often and says almost nothing, as though it wasn't his wedding they were planning, but someone else's entirely. Again and again, over side A and B of the cassette, Walt hears Tim clear his thick throat. He swears it sounds like thunder rumbling behind Rosie's voice full of pre-marriage optimism. If ambivalence makes a noise, this is it, Walt thinks, and he turns off the tape recorder with a jab of his thumb.

"You motherfucker," he mumbles, though he is not quite sure who he is naming.

Walt knows the tape isn't going to tell him what to do about his daughter's problems. After all, it didn't tell him that his adored dog was going to die two weeks after the tape was made, choked to death on a splintered pork chop bone dug out of the kitchen garbage. It didn't tell Walt that the reason he sometimes winced from pain as he held a pencil, or answered his wife irritably when he didn't mean to, was the onset of arthritis that wasn't going to go away.

As he puts the cassette back in its box, he knows that there's nothing really *to do* but let Rosie come back home for a while, as she wants. Helen has said yes, of course, immediately, come to us, we're here, but Walt already feels the burden of having her home again. He sees in the wrinkles of his face, his thinning hair, his thickening joints, a man who has no room for this sort of thing at the moment, a man who has no idea how much room is left at all. But Rosie is still his daughter, and he adores her, even if he doesn't feel like being anyone's father right now.

The following Tuesday, it is close to eight as Walt nears the Greyhound bus station, but the expressway is crowded even for a weekday in early December, and the traffic has stopped moving. Helen, on her way out to her reading group earlier, told him to take Cambridge Street downtown, but he's ignored her advice. Walt knows he'll be late meeting Rosie's bus from New York, and he worries about her in a familiar way. Rosie is twenty-five years old, has a job as a paralegal, an apartment on 73rd Street, a husband—is he still that? Someday she'll have kids. She's an independent person, he'd like to believe, but will she know enough to come and look outside for her father instead of expecting that he'll find her?

Walt remembers asking Rosie the same about Tim once: Does he know to meet us in your office? Meaning, is this man you're in love with, the one your mother is sure you'll marry just by the tone of your voice when you talk about him, capable of thinking of others? Walt had been in Manhattan for a conference at NYU. After lunch, he took a bus uptown to meet Rosie at work; Tim was supposed to meet them there too. As he watched the city through the sooty window, Walt found it hard to believe that his daughter lived in a place where there were so many things to do, to go wrong, and so many people to choose from. He carried in his briefcase a glass paperweight he'd bought for her in a store off Washington Square that morning.

Rosie's office was a small room off a hallway of other small rooms inhabited by women bent over papers or keyboards, fingering their earrings. She had a picture of her parents on her desk, which made Walt feel a little weak, and she put the paperweight next to it. When Tim didn't show up, and Walt and Rosie ran out of things to say after a while—easy without the clutter of the family—Rosie began to look miserable, her dark eyes watered, and she pulled hair loose from her ponytail. It was a habit she and her sister shared, as they shared their mother's thin face and his high forehead.

"I don't know, honey," Walt said gently, and looked at his watch, "maybe he thought we were going to meet him downstairs. Do you remember what you told him?" He hated it when his daughter acted stupid and here she was stupid about love, the worst of all things. It made him feel sorry for both of them.

Tim was on a bench in the building's courtyard, reclining long-legged and reading a book, when Walt and Rosie came out. He'd picked a spot shaded by a cherry tree in bloom, too beautiful for the city. Tim seemed content, so why should he think others wouldn't be, that they might be waiting for him.

"He doesn't have a watch," Rosie whispered to her father. She was clearly charmed by this, Walt saw, by her prince in a garden. Tim unfolded slowly to meet them. Rosie bounced on her tiptoes, her heels lifted out of her blue pumps, and Walt noticed she smelled a bit sweaty. She should be wearing red, rubber-tipped sneakers, he thought to himself, and approached Tim.

"Thought we were going to miss you," Walt said, and raised his eyebrows. It was a voice he often used with his students, a gentle challenge. The boy would not look at him. Tim's surprisingly handsome face was darkened by a two-day-old beard.

"No way," Tim said, and picked at the blossoms of the cherry tree. "Where do you want to go now?"

As if, Walt thought, this alone isn't enough for one father for one day, not to mention your dirty fingernails, your lack of a sense of time and expectations, your hold on my baby daughter. You'll take her away from me; I suppose I'll always dislike you for that. But he put his arm across Tim's shoulders, the way he had with his other daughter's boyfriend because he knew it would make Rosie happy.

"Whatever you two would like," Walt said, "is fine by me."

Later, when Walt told Helen about Tim, she laughed. "Pure jealousy," she'd said. "Fathers and their daughters. Rosie's a grown-up, let her go. You're the one who always says we baby her too much."

Mothers, Walt thinks now, looking for his daughter in the crowd bulging at the bus station entrance, accept when they have to, let go when they must, but watch out; they'll also turn their back on whoever hurts their child so quickly you'll feel the wind cut your face. Fathers, though, are rigid in the end; they suffer for their hearts that have been won so easily. Or is it my episodes of pain, Walt wonders, that's made my chest feel so tight lately?

He circles the station again but doesn't see Rosie in front. Now he'll be damned if he's going to look around for a parking place when it's cold and dark and he's in prime mugging territory. If Rosie really wants to come home so badly, she'll look outside for him. Walt pops one of his books-on-tape into the player and drives around the block—the traffic pattern is oval, with a light at each end. He's so engrossed by the true-life story of a baseball player (his other daughter gave it to him his last birthday) that it takes him a second to realize the person in the green parka trotting alongside the car and tapping at the window when he stops at a red light is Rosie, and not someone trying to take his car. She looks so much like his little girl, like both of his little girls at the point when their faces took their final beautiful shapes, her eyes bright with lack of understanding and the red Greyhound sign, that he wonders what year it is, and what year he'd like it to be.

When he unlocks the door, Rosie throws her duffel bag in the back seat. He can't help but be dismayed by the size of it, the amount of stuff she's packed for what he thinks is going to be a short visit home. She slips into the front seat and is slightly out of breath when Walt leans over and pulls her face to his lips. Her skin smells of diesel fumes and Jergens, Helen's lotion, so familiar he doesn't want to let her go. Walt notices that Rosie hasn't worn a hat and the tips of her ears are flaming cold, and he wants to touch them. Rosie seems lighthearted for the moment as they drive back to Cambridge, chatting about the bus ride, looking around at the familiar sights, avoiding any mention of Tim, or why she has come home. Walt again feels a touch of dismay at this, at how easily she can leave one thing and fall into another, like an experienced traveler crossing time zones.

He remembers driving four hours one July when she was thirteen to pick her up at camp mid-session. She was miserable, she'd said in her letters, she felt like she was in jail. The black flies by the lake were torture. Walt had glared at the camp director, his daughter's warden in khaki shorts, while Rosie had skipped— skipped!—off to her cabin to get her things, which naturally were not ready, as though this was a game. On the way home they'd stopped for lunch at a diner, and over grilled cheese and thick chocolate milk Rosie told him about the wonderful things she'd done for the past few weeks. He couldn't understand her changing from misery to delight so quickly. He felt his solitude shattered—the prospect of both girls away at the same time, just him and Helen alone—but also his loneliness abating.

"Got a couple of days off from work?" Walt asks. They are almost home, and he wants to know how long she'll be staying.

"Until Monday," she sighs, "but I may quit anyway. I'm not

crazy about the job." Walt knows by the way she's caught her breath that she's looking at his twisted hands on the steering wheel. When he looks down too, he sees rocks under his skin.

"Well, being crazy about something isn't always the standard to measure things by, Rosie. In fact, the older you get, the less good a standard it becomes." When he realizes how sad and defeated this sounds, he pats her on the knee and tells her that he's looking forward to spending time with her. "I'm really glad you're visiting."

During his standard end-of-the-semester lecture, Walt is aware of the wheels of the tape recorder that he's placed on the lectern going round and round, a tiny hiss only he can hear. He thinks of the letting out and taking up of the tape, and looks at Diana Lux's long legs in their black pants. She is in his sociology course on community structures, a small, bright head in the first row. Walt is not really listening to what he's saying—he can always rewind later to make sure he hasn't lost his rhythm, just his breath—but wondering if Diana still calls her parents Mommy and Daddy.

Rosie, who has been installed in her old room for a week now—the Monday to return to work come and gone—has taken to calling her parents Walt and Helen, has taken to phoning her older sister long distance every night. She emerges from her room after a conversation with Tim looking sleepy and red-eyed. Walt would like to call his daughter selfish and spoiled for the way she's descended upon them, but he calls her Rosita and Rosebud instead, and when she needs some money, or she asks him to get her a soda while he's up, he gives it to her. He sits with her at the kitchen table and they talk, they play Scrabble at night. She visited him at his office and they went to the Museum of Fine Arts, and afterward, at the gift shop, he bought her a silk scarf with a Matisse print on it.

The day after, when he woke in the morning, he felt as though his upper body was encased in cement. He called for his daughter down the hall. Helen had already left for work. Rosie drove him into Boston to the doctor's, dropped him off and parked the car so he wouldn't be late for the appointment. She was there when he finished, went with him to the pharmacy, and asked how he felt.

Her voice was wobbly with concern, so he showed her his new prescription for Auranofin. "These pills are made from gold extract," he told her. The doctor said they would slow the progression, a word Walt found particularly menacing. "If I take enough of them," he added, not to worry his daughter, "maybe you can melt me down into a pair of earrings."

Meanwhile, Helen has gone from salt to sugar, Walt notices, and hovers over Rosie's problems. Her mouth has stopped swelling; now she has pimples tiny as grains of sand and grease on the sides of her nose, and she talks a lot.

Diana Lux's face is so bright Walt can hardly stand it, and he looks down at his hands on the oak lectern. He would like Diana to tell him that he doesn't look old enough to have two grown women children, or that he's too old to have one tear at his heart, but he knows she's unlikely to be thinking anything so complex.

Rosie found a therapist in Cambridge, and tells her parents when she joins them for dinner in the kitchen. "I need a safe place right now," she says. Walt thinks she's looking thin and exotic dressed in black with her hair loose. Her earrings, though, are like something his secretary would wear, big gold globs, panic buttons. "She thinks I didn't feel safe with Tim."

"He didn't beat you up?" Helen says, half stating, half asking. They both hold their breath for her answer.

"No, of course not," Rosie says. All she's eaten is a breadstick, Walt sees, and he wonders why this detail takes up so much space in his head.

"Of course not? Is that so obvious?" he asks. His mouth is full of chicken and he swallows. "The way you ran out of there, I thought maybe he did hit you or something, maybe you're afraid to go back. *That* at least I can make sense of." He is very angry, and both women look a little scared of what's happening to him.

"It doesn't have to be physical abuse, Dad," she says. Helen nods. "There are other kinds." He wonders at her authority now as she talks with someone else's words.

He is Dad again suddenly. He remembers a time when his daughters came to him with stomachaches, and he could soothe them with a story. Later it was cramps that bothered them, they soothed each other, and stayed far away from him. It was like being fenced off from a place you used to live. He wanted to break back in.

"Please. In my day," he starts, and spews a fleck of food onto the table, "you didn't just leave because you didn't feel 'safe.' What is this shit anyway about safety? This has always been your problem, Rosie, you never feel you have to stick with anything, you can run home any time you like. Your mother and I are to blame for that too, I'll admit. You come, we take you in."

The women tilt their heads at similar angles.

"She's your daughter, for God's sake," Helen says. "Of course we take her in."

Walt sees that Rosie is close to tears. He puts his napkin on his plate—something he knows Helen hates—and leaves the table. In his study, he hears Helen and Rosie talking in the kitchen, and thinks how easily Helen has become a complete mother again, how little she fights this return. Walt feels bad for what he's said but justified in saying it. In a while, he puts in the cassette from his afternoon's lecture.

He can't believe that the voice he hears is his own, and he adjusts the tone on the machine. He sounds flat, dated is how he really thinks of it, the voice of a half-asleep man. From time to time, a staccato cough punctuates his drone, and he imagines that it's Diana Lux trying to rouse him and get his attention, even at this moment in the privacy of his own home, calling him to imagine her in her dorm room in her flannel pajamas. He pictures her tumbling like a gymnast over futons and beanbag chairs, like a doll with string joints.

The light from the kitchen blinds him momentarily. "What are you doing?" Helen asks. It's not accusatory, just curious.

"Listening to today's lecture," he says. "Do you think my voice sounds funny?"

She puts her fingers to her lips. Being married to him for so many years has made her a good listener. "Not really, a little nasal maybe. Why, do you?"

"I thought it sounded flat. Old."

Helen sits on the arm of his chair. She smells like dish soap and chocolate. "Maybe you need new batteries."

He pats her leg in wool pants. "Maybe *you* need new batteries," he jokes.

Helen smiles and gets up to straighten a picture on the wall. It happens, by chance, to be one of Rosie at twelve, knocked slightly askew by the swiveling arm of his desk lamp.

"In my day . . ." Helen starts, doing her imitation of Walt, putting her head down on her chest so that a double chin appears and her eyebrows meet, ". . . in my day . . ." She stops, looks at him, and talks in her own voice. "In your day, Walt? My day and your day are the same, remember? You didn't have that day—and what day was it, anyway?—without me." Walt shrugs.

"Rosie's talking to Tim," Helen adds, matter-of-factly. How easily we pass these things by, Walt thinks, and feels affection for his wife and his long marriage. They've never talked about what will happen if one day he can't move anymore.

"Yes? And what's this about her finding a shrink here? That has the ring of long-term," Walt says. "Doesn't she have to go home at some point? What about her job? And what the hell is she doing about her marriage? Isn't that the problem at hand, as they say?"

Now Helen shrugs, and Walt knows that she too would really like to be done with this—after all, for several years they've been living a different kind of life—but can't bring herself to say so, won't allow herself. Rosie has always been trouble in one way or another, a baby is always—lovely, painful trouble.

"And since we're talking about marriage, how's ours?" he asks and holds his arms open to her. It's as close as he can come to apologizing at the moment.

"I'm not really thinking about it," Helen says, which doesn't surprise or hurt him. She holds his hands, and can't help but massage them a little. "I'm thinking about Rosie now, what she's going to do." Before she leaves the room, Helen kisses his forehead and reminds him to take his gold pills.

Walt has been told by Helen that Tim is coming up from New York Tuesday evening, but on the day he pretends he's forgotten and stays at work and eats dinner at the Faculty Club. He hopes Diana Lux will appear at his late office hours. When she doesn't, he thinks spitefully about giving her a C for the semester—she is mediocre at best. When he gets home just after nine, Helen's car is gone, and he remembers it's her reading group night. This means that now he'll actually have to talk to Tim instead of letting Helen buffer for him, excuse her husband's behavior. The house is warm and dark and smells like tomato soup, and in fact, when he goes into the kitchen, that's just what the smell is. Two empty bowls, skimmed with red, bisected by spoons, are on the table uncleared. Walt smells Tim too, salty and male, and thinks how much fathers are like dogs.

By the time Walt reaches the top of the stairs, he can hear that his daughter and her husband are at it—he can't bring himself to think making love or even fucking at that moment—and the sounds are so easy for him to make out, he's at first delighted by his acuity and then horrified by it. Has he ever listened to other people—Jesus, his daughter!—making love except in the movies? She giggles, he groans, long breaths are let out and grabbed back in. The duet has the most incredible, indescribable fluid life, and he can't bear it.

He reaches into his blazer pocket for the recorder he always carries in case he wants to tape random thoughts or reminders, or just the noise of what happens. If you didn't know who or what was making the sounds behind the door, would you know what it was? he wonders. He thinks of a radio contest he used to listen to as a boy where you tried to identify certain sounds—a sewing machine whirring, crackers being broken, a cat licking herself. Can I pretend this is not my daughter, he thinks now, but just noise too? Would you know it wasn't love?

Walt turns the recorder on and lays it on the rug outside the door. He sits in his bedroom in the dark, sliding toward the floor on the slippery bedspread, and waits until it is quiet. Then he retrieves the machine, its red ON light like a rat's eye in the dark hall.

"Dad?" Rosie says from inside as he picks it up. He is frozen in a painful crouch and wonders if he'll be able to rise again. Her voice sounds full, as though her throat has been opened.

"Oh, hi," Walt says, straining, not to be defeated. He can just imagine Tim, arms behind his head, bare-chested, hairy armpits, staring at the ceiling. "It's late, sweetheart. I'll see you in the morning." He makes a point of shutting his bedroom door loudly, just as he's made a point not to acknowledge Tim.

When Helen comes home and upstairs, Walt says he has a surprise for her. A small smile crosses her face—at fifty-three, she does want to believe in good surprises still, miracle cures. When he plays the tape for her, her eyes widen as though she's spotted something across the room and leans toward it. She is holding the book from her group against her chest.

"Guess," Walt says. "Guess what it is."

"What is this? Jesus Christ," she says, and rushes for the recorder, but she can't immediately find the button to turn it off, and for a second, turns up the volume. "This is sick, really crazy," she says, but hands the machine back to Walt and sits down on the bed next to him. "What are you doing?" she pleads.

"I don't want them fucking in my house," he says, firmly. "If she doesn't love him, she shouldn't be fucking him either. Should I have to listen to this?"

"Oh, Walt," Helen moans. "You sound like an old man." Her eyes narrow. "Rosie doesn't know what she wants. They're married, they're adults, they're allowed not to know. No one made you listen."

"They should go home."

Helen shakes her head at him. "Why are you doing this?" She is disappointed and crying when she says, "Don't make us hate you."

The next morning Helen leaves early to teach a class, and when Walt goes downstairs for coffee, Rosie and Tim are at the kitchen table, posed over empty bowls again, their dark heads together. He sees that Tim's bare feet are resting on top of Rosie's under the table. Walt cannot bring himself to talk directly to them, but says a general hello to the room, and touches his daughter on the shoulder as he makes his way to the stove. Tim says hi. Rosie, still in her bathrobe, doesn't say anything. She is not capable of hurting her father. Walt wonders if Helen has told them something, warned them about him, and the shame of what he's done, what he's listened to, makes him back away quickly.

"I'm going to be working here today," he announces, and moves into his study. "So . . . I guess I'll see you." An hour later, his other daughter calls, but she wants to talk to Rosie and not to him, and he wonders how far his poison has spread. By mid-afternoon Walt can't stand the whispering between Tim and Rosie, both the urging and the caressing that's gone on for hours, and he goes to his office.

Several days later, Diana Lux comes to Walt's office to discuss why her term paper is going to be late. He admires her for not lying to him, but simply telling him that it's late because she didn't start it early enough. He commends her parents for teaching her honesty and self-reliance, although at the moment he finds it extremely unappealing. He makes his hands into a pyramid on top of his desk. She doesn't appear to notice the almost purple hue to his skin.

"Fine," Walt says. Diana's sweatshirt has *University of Wisconsin* on it. They are nowhere near Wisconsin, and Walt suspects it's where her boyfriend goes to school, a big-chested blond sort of guy. "Drop it off in my box when you're finished."

"That's okay?" She's done something strange to her hair, so

that her bangs point to the ceiling. She sits like a ballerina, with only her pointed toes touching the floor. He doesn't answer her. "Really?"

I'm not your father, Walt thinks, furious, and damned if I'm going to have to say it twice to reassure you and make you feel good about yourself, good about screwing up but being honest about it.

"It's up to you," he says, coldly. "It's your decision, your grade."

Walt knows that she thinks she's been pardoned, when he's done nothing of the sort for her.

Later, when he straightens the papers on his desk before going home, he sees that Diana has left her pen. It's a fake fat tortoise-shell thing, with bite marks on the cap. He can't help thinking that her father must have given it to her as he sent her away, and that now she feels she's really lost something important to her, all her good luck and love in that cheap pen. He doesn't understand how the pen got on his desk unless she put it there, and he can't remember her moving toward him.

When Walt gets home, he knows that Tim has gone. He also knows that Rosie is still in the house; she has not gone with him. He can't understand why people act like this, so inconclusive with their own lives, so dependent on other people to hold them up, but if anyone's to blame for Rosie being like that, he supposes that he is—he is her father. He sees Helen is home too, early, that life in his house is taking place without him.

When he calls for Helen and Rosie, ready to be forgiven—he's sick, he's scared, he'll tell them, he's hateful and he hates his body—they don't answer. He feels a terrible need to be included.

Upstairs, he hears voices again behind a closed door, this time in the bathroom. The water is running into the clawfoot tub, and he listens to Helen and Rosie talking quietly to each other. When he puts his hand out to touch the door, he swears he can feel the steam that clouds the bathroom, then Rosie's little sobs and sniffs, and Helen's comfort that finally shakes the house.

He pushes the door open the smallest bit. He wants to witness as well as hear for once, and sees Helen sitting on a stool next to the tub. Rosie's head is resting against her mother's thigh, while one hand trails along the edge, her fingers dripping water onto the floor. They don't notice him there, and he doesn't want to be seen.

Walt suddenly remembers a photograph he saw in *Life* years before, black-and-white, of a Japanese mother bathing her deformed and half-grown child in a wooden tub. There was no pleasure on either of their faces, but it wasn't displeasure or pain either, which had surprised him. The girl's hands were stiff claws, unable to hold the cloth, and her mother had to keep the hair back from her child's eyes. He had stared at the picture without understanding why. Back then he had simply shut the magazine and put it away. Now he admits to himself what he had been thinking about: that if the child had died, or if her mother had chosen not to care for her, to keep her, then there would be no bath, there would be no moment.

Walt is crying as he shuts the door and goes downstairs into his study. In a while, he hears that the water has been turned off in the bathroom and the drain opened to let it out. In a gush, it rushes down from the second floor, down through the pipes that run through the wall of his study, splashing toward the sewer below him. It's a warm sound, warm as Helen wrapping a towel around Rosie, warm as he wrapped his last baby in a blanket and held her to his chest, warm as though the water's running over him. It sounds too much like life being washed out of his house, and he can't imagine there ever being a time when he'd want to hear it again.

Our daughter Emma has lined up the goods on the kitchen table like wedding presents for her father who is coming home today. I'm surprised what people give a man with only one hand—a flack jacket with twelve zippers is the latest arrival. At six years old, Emma seems to understand half of everything, and chooses not to understand the rest, and so she's unwrapped each one of the gifts for Ellis because she knows he can't do that part himself. But I wonder, as I watch her straighten and rearrange this endless supply of stuff, why she doesn't understand that the only way her father may ever be able to close a zipper is with his teeth.

It seems like forever she's been opening these gifts Ellis's friends keep dropping by. Do they actually believe accumulation is part of a cure for loss, both his and mine? Emma is particularly eager to get everything just so right now, but there have been false alarms for Ellis's return before, and I'm half expecting today to offer up another one. At this point, Emma knows that we might drive to the hospital at the top of the hill, park in front, and then have to leave without her father. She knows how we'll force a cheeriness on each other on the ride back and decide to stop at the bookstore for a new book or tape to take up that immediate

17

emptiness when we get home. Last time, I wouldn't let her get a make-your-own calendar kit. It was already one month into the new year, I explained, and it would be a waste to have only eleven left to color and plaster with pony stickers. The truth is, I've wanted to hide everything from her about days and weeks and the excruciating tedium of Ellis's body and my pride struggling to heal themselves.

I tell her it's time to get her sweater and brush her hair; we have to leave soon. I wonder anxiously why it is the doctors never spot the problem, the infection, the fever of unknown origin *before* we get there, why they never call and save me the trip and the traffic on Eddy Street, but more important, the wear and tear on our hearts. Three times it's been the same thing, and I can't hear any more about setbacks and nerve damage because at a certain point the specifics don't matter. All I can think about is how I've ended up with a husband who has emptied me out and a daughter who is so optimistic—now she bounds into the room, all shiny-haired and eager—it makes me want to weep.

When we go into his room, Ellis is sitting on the bed. He's fully dressed, which is further than he's ever gotten in all this time, and it's an unsettling sight. His plaid flannel shirt which had been hanging in the room's closet has been buttoned all the way up, making him look like a prisoner. Ellis has always boasted of his imperviousness to the cold, and so I know he would never have done up the shirt like this, even if he could. Nurse Jeannie, or Nurse May Luc, has done it for him. These women love him like everyone else does, love his compliments and teases and flirtations. At the end of their shifts, I'm sure they rush home to repeat something remarkable he has said.

They have also pulled my husband's socks up, tied his hiking boots, buckled his belt, combed and flattened his hair as if he were a child, and not fifty-five. His beard has been trimmed, showing more than usual of its gray. During the almost four weeks he's been in the hospital—add a bonus one for a spiking fever that had him babbling and purple-faced—I've gotten unsolicited lectures about the importance of maintaining the accident victim's pride. Even with one arm amputated mid-forearm, the other sporting a thumb and two-fingered mangle of a bruised hand, my husband is the picture of pride today. If these advice-givers know the details of Ellis's accident—he was with another woman, but I am his wife—they don't let on, a powerful humiliation for me. They can barely look me in the eye, yet they dare to explain that Ellis—that we, for God's sake—are simply the recipients of the random fall of bad luck.

I've come to understand that what a hospital loathes the most is not death, or even illness, but disorder, and this morning Ellis is, at least on the outside, as orderly as a man with his problems can be. But inside, threatening disorder reigns. There is dysaesthesia, a misalignment of healing nerves in his remaining hand, and his range of motion is disappointing. Pinch is what we're after, I'm told, and he's not showing any progress toward that simple human necessity. Pinch a cheek, a cracker off a plate, a bud off a bush, pinch yourself. Ellis's hand is as stiff as steel and if it gets any worse he'll lose this one as well, but today he's coming home.

"My daddy," Emma says and climbs onto his lap. They begin their private conversation. A man Ellis's age can only adore his only child.

"Lise," Ellis calls to me. When I bend to kiss him, he tries to put his tongue in my mouth. I feel Emma's hair against my cheek, and I know the three of us together is her idea of heaven, but the only thing I can think is that I'm offended, terribly and horribly offended by what Ellis is doing. If he had hands instead of a puckered stump and the claw he's hidden under his thigh, he would have gathered me to him and it might have been comforting. But he holds me in a different way now, and if I pull away I will damage his soul and I'm not sure I can do that, despite everything, so I stay and ease into the force of his kiss.

"My two girls," Ellis says, his eyes a little watery and still on me, trying to see what he's gained in these last few minutes. "Take me home. Let's blow this pop stand." Emma laughs herself off his lap. "Let's blow this joint," he bellows. Emma is delighted, squeaks the toes of her boots on the floor, shimmies her hips. She is in love with her father, and tonight she'll have to sleep in her own bed, a thought which fills me with dread for both of us. "This hellhole, this snake pit, this cesspool, this party." Ellis never knows when to stop—he'll hold people hostage until past midnight with his stories. "This fucking boneyard," he yells, stirring Emma into a frenzy of giggles.

"Let's go," I say, and hook my arm through what's left of Ellis's. He's vulnerable and wouldn't be able to break his fall if he had to. "The car's in front."

"I love you," he whispers to me and then turns to Emma. "Hey, Em, help me look for my hand, will you? I can't seem to find it anywhere. Try under the bed."

"Oh Dad," she sighs, playing along. She chews the end of her hood string. "You left it in the road, remember? How many times do I have to tell you?"

"You're right again," he thrills her by saying.

Ellis stumbles a little as we step out of the hospital, but I have him. He takes his first breath of unfiltered air in weeks, and his eyes tear again. I don't know whether this is from the exhaust swirling around us or real sunlight in the cold, or from something else. "Careful," I tell him, as he gets into the front seat of our ancient car, and Emma hops into the back. Ellis has lost some weight, which makes this maneuvering easier, but it's still awkward. "Here, let me do that for you," I offer, and lean over him to buckle the seat belt.

"I have a feeling we're going to be hearing that a lot," he says to me. Bitterness is in his voice though he's smiling. "Maybe we should just have a button installed which you can push instead of having to repeat yourself."

"I want one," Emma says, but unlike her, I'm not sure how to respond. My head is just about at Ellis's chest while I struggle to straighten out the seat belt.

Eight years ago, when we met, Ellis said I needed to be touched, and he was right; I'd been alone and unhappy. I decided I could love him and overlook his two previous marriages, his women in between. I decided I could overlook the infidelities he told me about as something that had already happened before I appeared. I could see my way around his twelve years on me, his tendency to get drunk too often and too enthusiastically, his proprietary best friend Paul, his life in place while I was still trying to find mine. Ellis said he had made a discovery when he found me, and that with my blond hair and big bones I reminded him of something from a St. Lucia's Day festival. He made me think my wide thighs and white skin, dense and doughy, could be as satisfying as warm sweet rolls. Of course, I recognized even then the drama of his seduction, but at thirty-four I wanted a man and a baby both to hold. I cannot explain the core of this longing any better today as I feel Ellis next to me in the car, and my head is still down so close to him. It is just that, a core, deep in, blind to the outside.

Now my husband could be on a respirator, peeing into a bag, fed through a tube. He could be in a wheelchair, in diapers and drooling, sensing I looked only vaguely familiar, staring at his daughter like a deranged man, scaring her out of her mind. The son of a bitch could be dead, too, but he isn't, and I notice that he still smells like Ellis, despite the hospital's sterility. I want to wail how much I loved him once, and now I'll have to leave, but I have been without him for so long his scent overpowers me and such troubling declarations.

After our wedding, I moved into Ellis's house in Fox Point, a short walk from his studio and the art school where he taught furniture making. I was charmed by the place, which had been built for a preacher in 1895. The rooms were small but long, imitations of a tiny church, and the ceilings were unusually high so the Reverend could be closer to God. Ellis made a studio for me in the garage, which wasn't ever big enough for a car anyway, and later, with some money left to him when his father died, Ellis built an oddly angled covered walkway from the house to the studio that traversed our small, clotted yard.

Out of something he swore was called monkey-wood, he created a beautiful carved archway for me to walk through. Its color was more reddish than brown, and the grain swirled with tiny, twisting knots. I invited people, all friends of Ellis's I was just getting to know at the time, to come over and see it. I boasted of how much my husband loved me, and how I'd been lifted up from my past life and gently put down in the place where I was meant to be. The friends left their admiring fingerprints on the monkey-wood and turned so I couldn't see their faces while I went on and on behind them.

Then, a room for our baby was cleared, more and more space for her toys, a corner for her plastic stove and sink set. After years together, Ellis still referred to the change we brought to his life as the "invasion," and pictured himself a pacified heathen among the toy and Tampax mercenaries.

Two weeks after Ellis's accident, while he was still in the hospital, I paid a disability consultant to come to the house and tell me what needed to be done. My friends talked about how brave I was to face reality, plan for the future, and stop weeping in bed. I'd only considered myself practical to do this much for Ellis before I left him. The consultant drank a cup of coffee while standing up, and started to tell me about her son, victim of a DWI, until I was so depressed I lied and told her I had bad cramps and needed to go to bed with some massive painkillers. I just didn't have a whole lot of sympathy left.

Later, Ellis's friend Paul helped me change the light switches to big plastic buttons you can turn on and off with an elbow or a prosthesis. I watched as he hooked up an electric foot-operated device that raises and lowers the toilet seat—a must, the consultant had said. (Why, with his balding head inches from the bowl, did Paul tell me how much Ellis loved me, as though that meant anything?) I've already had the thing fixed once because Emma's been playing with it, forcing it up and down against its will. I hear it whining at night in my sleep, Emma up and restless, but I'm too tired to stop her.

Only now, on this day we've brought Ellis home and he stands in the middle of the kitchen, do I see how little all I've done amounts to. Ellis is describing the gadgets in an authoritative way—I haven't heard this loud a voice in the house in a month—as Emma touches each one like a game show hostess. He's right, though: they are obvious and ugly against wide honeyed planks and deep rose walls, a further assault to the handicapped, he declares. I realize too, as he does, that being able to turn on lights and lift the toilet seat means almost nothing. They are instant, not prolonged activities like sipping coffee or turning the pages of a book, or even scratching a mosquito bite until you bleed. In this first hour, I've already opened doors for Ellis, put on his slippers and a sweater, pulled up his pants and buckled his belt, and now I think he's afraid to sit because he might not be able to get up himself and he'll be forced to ask me for one more thing. He has to go back to the hospital on Monday for physical and occupational therapy, so it occurs to me that he might not sit until then, he'll stand all weekend. I picture him silvered in the sad, winter moonlight, and the reality of his helplessness—and it will only get worse if he loses the hand—is suddenly overwhelming.

"How about some lunch?" I offer, weakly.

"Actually, I'm not very hungry," Ellis says, "but I'd take some orange juice if you had any."

"Me too," Emma agrees. Her face looks expectant but strained. My hand is on the refrigerator door and suddenly I'm so angry I'm shaking. "If *I* have any?" My voice catches roughly in my mouth. "Don't you mean if *we* have any? You're not a guest, Ellis. You're home, so don't talk like you don't live here."

My husband can't pour, or do anything for himself—and we both know it. "I might as well be a guest, don't you think?"

"Just tell me how I should do this," I say, and take out the juice. I am ashamed to look at Emma now. "A straw, right?" I've bought the box of 1,000, assorted colors. I have another box in the basement, stockpiled for his future.

"Right, a straw would be good, and then you can just put it

down," he instructs. Ellis has learned some tricks at the hospital, and now he'll have to teach them to me. He sits and I push him in, but the joints of the wooden chair—one of a beautiful, delicate set he made—protest loudly.

Emma tries to crawl on her father's lap, ignoring his discomfort as she bumps and jostles his hand—and he can't say no. The pain on his face is too much, too much the martyr's now, and finally I have to lift Emma up from under the arms to get her off. She drops her weight suddenly, I feel my back strain dangerously and that terrible, instant impulse to slap her.

Emma and I have been alone together for a month, our needs have often merged, and now she looks at me as though I've betrayed her. "But it's Dad's lap," she cries, "not yours."

In the meantime, silent in the storm that is his daughter, Ellis has managed to sweep the glass toward himself and fit his lips around the straw. He looks up to see us staring at him.

"Okay, we've got to have a few rules here," he says, after swallowing. "First, rule number one: no staring at me, because you're going to see some pretty ugly things if you look too hard—and anyway, it makes me nervous." He does that quick, teasing lift of his eyebrows. "It takes me about an hour to blow my nose."

"Gross," Emma says, wiping her tears.

"If you think that's gross, you should see me try to pick it."

Ellis goes back to his juice while I pretend to busy myself in the kitchen but actually stare out the window. Emma, off in the other room—never a child to be alone, except now suddenly—has put in a babyish lullaby tape we haven't listened to in years. Ellis hums to it, off-key, and I wonder what memory he's using to soothe himself. Over the fence lives a woman who feeds the birds in her nightgown at all hours, and for a second I consider telling him that she's there now, in her brand-new flannel; he'd get a kick out of the peppermint stripes and bows at her neck, her red rubber boots. The woman casts a quick eye at the back of our house, and I shiver as Ellis sucks up that last bit of orange juice. And what will we do now, what are we waiting for?

"Well," Ellis says, and I hear his feet sliding on the floor, "it's good to be back."

A raccoon has spilled over one of the garbage cans, and I can't ask Ellis to go out and clean up the orange peels scattered on the snow. "You were gone a long time."

"I know it's supposed to be the other way around, but the place seems so big. And I didn't remember this room being so light."

"Is that right?" I respond. "Hmm."

"That's right." He might bang the table for emphasis now if he could. "You did a lot, with those light switches and everything," he says. "Thanks."

I want to tell him how my plan was to arrange things so he could take care of himself, by himself, and how impossibly short of the mark I've fallen. "It's hard to know where to start."

"The can's good," he assures me. "You know men and their bathrooms." He laughs and expects me to laugh with him. The vagueness of our conversation scares me, as if we did all our talking in the hospital. I don't want to cry, but I do.

"Come here, Lise," he coaxes, but I turn on the water as if I haven't heard him. "It's okay." I hear his glass moving across the table, as though he's pushing it back and forth in the bend of his arm. "I'm home. Things are going to be fine, we're going to work it out. When this hand gets better, I'll be able to do everything—okay, almost everything—for myself. And then for you."

"No, it's not fine," I say. Ellis thinks this is consoling, and that he, back in this house, is some kind of consolation for what he's lost us. For him, the accident is over, his body is clear enough proof of it. But for me, I realize, it's as though it hasn't even happened yet.

I've invited Paul over for Ellis's second night back and we're sitting in the living room. Ellis is drinking a beer with a Krazy straw Paul gave him as a welcome home present, and I'm having a glass of wine. It's not an unusual picture, the three of us sitting and drinking and talking, with Emma asleep upstairs (she didn't fight when I put her in her own bed this time), and the familiarity is of course why I have chosen it. I am exhausted, and could give in to listening to their gossipy conversation where they left off before the accident, but tonight I can't let myself. Ellis, having a good time, asks for another beer and Paul eagerly opens one for him.

I look at Ellis rocking in his favorite chair, beer can balanced confidently on the wide arm, and it strikes me, not for the first but for the thousandth time, how much I don't know about his accident, though I've spent some terrible hours imagining it. I do know that Ellis had gone to an art opening in Boston with three of his studio students. Two of them were in the back of the Honda when they picked Ellis up; an empty seat was left for him in front. It's always been understood that he's the one to get the rides—an accident years before we met left Ellis with a dislike of driving. He could drive, but he didn't, and he'd arranged his life within walking distance.

Emma and I watched the car as it drove away that evening last month, my husband already turned to flatter the girl in the driver's seat whose profile was so striking in the roof light. I can say now that what I felt then was a premonition—and a premonition is really nothing but a sign to prepare for what you haven't yet admitted is inevitable—but at the time it felt like something closer to acceptance.

At that moment—the car with Ellis gone, the street dark again—I told myself that my marriage, stretching into its eighth year, probably wasn't all that I imagined it was, but up close, what ever is? I had Emma pressed against my front, her head just above my belly. I loved her so completely, I decided that was a lot for one life, possibly enough. She was ours, we were hers, and Ellis was everyone's. Oddly, I was happy—or not unhappy—and simply enormously grateful for her head resting in my hands.

Later, after I'd put Emma to bed, I went to my studio to do some drawing for a textbook job I'd gotten, stroked the monkey-wood arch, and worked until the phone rang from the emergency room at New England Medical Center.

"Lise Warton? You're his wife?" they asked.

He was in surgery already. He'd lost a hand, they were doing what they could with the other. The girl—yes, just the two of them in the car, as far as they knew—had a few stitches in her forehead. Did I know how to get hold of her parents? *Her parents?* I drove like a crazy person to Paul's, where I deposited a dazed daughter. I smoked half a pack of stale cigarettes I found in the glove compartment before I'd even reached Boston, and I'd bent over my heavily sedated husband in the hospital. I waited for his hand to rise and stroke my cheek, but it didn't.

"Oh Lise," Ellis managed to mumble after several hours of my ferocious vigil over him. "You're here. Fucking cars, you know? Oh baby, they took my hand. What am I going to do with only one hand?"

Now I noisily rearrange myself on the couch, and Paul, who is sitting next to me, straightens up. "That girl," I say to Ellis, "the one who was in the accident with you, the one who was driving. She ever visit you in the hospital?"

I don't care about the girl at all, but I'm stuck with the image of my husband's mouth on her breast, and he's making a humming sound as he caresses her. It's a noise I once felt flowing through my body.

Ellis looks up at me, the straw still in his mouth. He has to let it slide out from between his lips and dive through the thickness of the beer before he can talk. "I don't remember."

"How can you not know? Either she did or she didn't. You lost a hand, you didn't go blind." I really have no more nice things to say to Ellis; I must have said them all in the hospital, always so sympathetic from my plastic visitor's chair. I can feel Paul shifting uncomfortably next to me.

"Because I had a lot of visitors," Ellis answers, patiently. "Students, friends, and I was doped up a lot of the time. Maybe she did come, I just don't remember."

"Jesus, what time is it? I have to go," Paul says, and stands up. For once, Ellis does not try to get him to stick around for another beer. "Hey, I'd walk you out, but I might not be able to get back in by myself," Ellis yells from the other room when we're by the front door.

Paul laughs back and touches my cheek. I really hate his soft ways, how short he is, and how his voice changes when he speaks to me. "Lise, he loves you so much."

"Stop saying that," I demand, and push his hand away. "Stop patronizing me. How many times are you going to say he loves me?"

Once, a couple of years ago, Paul slept with Ellis's second ex-wife—I don't know what he and Ellis do with this ugly fact between them. "Okay, look. I know how tough this is on you," Paul says, "but it's tough on him too. He lost his hand, his work, a whole lot. He's scared. Go easy, that's all I'm saying. He just got home."

"That means I'm not supposed to ask him about the accident? I have a right to know."

"But what difference does it make? All these questions about the girl. Pretend he was going out to get some milk if you have to, because that's about how important it was. You'd accept *that*, wouldn't you? Christ, you should be glad he's alive. He's your husband."

But Ellis wasn't acting as my husband, wasn't thinking as my husband when he dumped our lives into this shallow pit, and that's the difference. "Just go home," I say to Paul, and open the door for him.

Ellis has made his way upstairs, and when I come into the bedroom, he's sitting on the bed. "I'm supposed to do my exercises," he informs me.

"Tonight? It's after midnight."

"Hey, I'm just trying to save my hand here, okay?" he snaps. His pain, he is suggesting, is another issue.

And so I bring over the economy size of Nivea cream the doctor told me to buy, and I retrieve the red rubber ball from the Patient Belongings bag still in the corner. I begin to massage his hand.

I've done this before in the hospital, kneeling in front of him, so I'm not squeamish at the way his skin folds like wet linen.

Ellis's flesh seems loose around the bones and his fingers feel saw-edged as I roll them between my palms. "Did she visit you or not?"

"Not," he says, and draws his breath in.

I can't do anything to loosen his hand up—his palm is closed as a shell. He'll never ever hold this red ball. "Try to pinch it," I urge, slipping my finger between his like a wedge. "A little pinch."

"I can't," he winces. All this manipulation clearly hurts him a lot, more than it should. His eyes have a drawn-back look. "Stop."

I begin to undress Ellis. As I pull his pants off, his penis jolts a little when I brush it with my hand, and he clears his throat—ashamed, I think. Though he asks me not to, I undress with the lights out. I am bent under the low ceiling; the Reverend did not need to be closer to God in his bedroom. In the middle of the night, I wake to find myself both very hot and very cold. Ellis has somehow managed to contort himself to fit his lower half around mine and we're sweating together. But his upper half is uncovered, so that his hand can hang off the far side of the bed, banished to sleep alone.

Finally it's Monday, and we're stuck in traffic on the Point Street Bridge. It's been a morning of bad timing; Ellis waited for me to dress him, to brush his teeth, to feed him the fruity bits of his yogurt that wouldn't fit through the straw. He made a joke about being the second child I always wanted. He waited while I ran in to Emma's school with her. He doesn't want to be late for his appointments this morning, he says again. He's going to whip this hand of his back into shape.

First, Ellis is supposed to see Martha in Physical Therapy, then James in Occupational. He is wearing a knapsack—the single useful gift he was given, though he can neither put it on nor take it off himself—and in it he's carrying some presents: a bright pink port wine cheese ball and some Italian jelly candies for these people who are his new friends. As usual, the traffic around the hospital is heavy too, and both the first and second lots are full.

"The trouble with hospitals," he says, as I circle for a space. "Too many sick people."

"I bet we could get some handicapped plates. No more parking troubles for the rest of our lives."

Ellis's face tightens. "Just drop me by the front."

I see that I've zipped his jacket up too high, and the teeth are cutting into the skin at his neck. He looks toward the hospital, and I know he can't wait to get out of the car. "I'll just go around once or twice more," I say. "Plenty of time."

"You don't have to come in with me." Ellis is beginning to sound a little desperate.

"I think I should."

Ellis sighs. "Later, maybe. Jesus, Lise, not today, please. I don't want you to come with me yet. I don't want you to see me trying to feed myself and spilling down my front, or trying to wipe my own ass, okay?" He pauses. "I couldn't stand it."

"I'm humiliated too, you son of a bitch. Think of it as something we have in common." I drive to the front. "This all right?" I don't move to help him out. In a minute, I've cruelly forced him to say he can't undo the belt or open the door without my help.

When I'm home, Ellis calls from the hospital. He's going to walk back, he informs me, he needs the exercise, and he'll pick Emma up at school on his way. I know he'll be an hour early getting there, even if he walks slowly across the bridge and up Wickenden Street. He may be hoping to run into a friend or a former student who'll invite him to go someplace for coffee with a straw.

I had intended to work while he was gone, but I can't make myself go through the archway this morning, so I clean and pick up instead. I throw out Emma's socks that are missing their mates, I consolidate the slew of tea bags on the kitchen shelf. I do some laundry; Ellis's dirty clothes smell dirty in a different way now. By noon I am exhausted from useless activity.

At two-thirty I'm standing by the window for any sign of my husband and daughter. I have started this lookout early—it's all I can do not to troll around in my car—and I know they'll be late, walking slowly, dodging snow mounds and puddles. I don't think I've ever stood so still, and forty minutes later I see Ellis and Emma coming around the corner. Even from this distance, I can tell Emma is chattering away and thrilled to be with her father. There is a child in her class with a botched cleft-palate repair, another with psoriasis migrating across his cheeks, and so she's taken her father's deformities with great equanimity.

Ellis's hand is pulled up into the sleeve of his jacket so that no skin is bared to the cold, and Emma keeps reaching behind for him. That I've taught her to be so reflexively cautious when it's time to cross the street seems particularly painful right now. But she won't give up, finally takes a step back and simply grabs for Ellis's hand deep within the sleeve. She has refused to understand that she can reach for him but there is nothing to hold or protect her. Ellis lets out a yowl that slices right through the glass of the window I'm pressed against and forces me to take a step back. Oh, my poor, beautiful daughter, frozen for a second and then bursting into tears which give her enough momentum to come flying up the street, *Lion King* knapsack slapping her back, and into my arms where I'm waiting for her on the shitty sidewalk in only my socks. She is trembling, covered with slush, terrified she's hurt her father.

Ellis is red-faced and sweating when he comes inside after taking an extra twenty minutes around the neighborhood. Emma is drinking chocolate milk with his Krazy straw. She doesn't look up when I go to answer her father's quiet pounding on the door.

I wait for Ellis to say something, and when he just stands there, unable even to take off his own coat, I start in on him. "How could you do that?" I scream. "You terrified her, you couldn't control yourself." When he doesn't respond, I aim my fists at his chest and hit Ellis so hard he stumbles back against the wall. "She waited an entire month for you to come, she loves you so much, and then you disappoint her like this? I can't bear it, what you've done to her." Ellis won't look at me. "Talk to her," I demand, "you tell her it isn't her fault, she didn't hurt you."

"But she did hurt me," he says softly and helplessly. "You can't believe how much, actually. This hand is shit, it's all wrong."

I want to hit him again, but he has not moved to protect himself from me. "God, I hate you."

"Why don't you leave me?" Ellis whispers. Emma can hear us, just as we can hear her pencils dropping on the floor. "Why would you stay with me, Lise?"

This—the way he understands it—takes my breath away and I can't answer him. Ellis stops in the kitchen to kiss Emma on the top of the head, but he seems unable to speak and makes his tired way up the narrow back stairs. His weight bumps against the walls, as though he's still reeling from my punch. In a while, when I go up, I find him on the bed, on his back, asleep. In all this, I cannot stand that his shoes are still on—he has refused to let me buy him elastic laces—and this seems like the greatest defeat, a sign of pure helplessness. When I begin to take them off for him, he manages to thank me. Then he moves his half arm across his face, and that's it.

Later, I hear him pacing around, and something glass breaking. It doesn't matter what it was or whether or not it was on purpose. Emma, fortunately, can't hear a thing because she's sitting ten inches away from the television, and alternately chewing on her hair and pretzels. She's still a little trembly despite the fact that I've hugged her much of the afternoon and assured her that Ellis is okay.

It's been a week, and Ellis continues to go to the hospital alone, one of the few things he can do without me. There is nothing else for him to do during the day except this walk, he says. He has already postponed the meeting at work to discuss his future. He claims he has none. In the afternoons he makes bread with Emma when they get home. This involves her measuring out the ingredients at his instruction, dumping them into the well of the bread machine, and having her press the ON button. They take turns checking the progress, and when the machine is in knead mode Ellis leans against the counter, feeling the vibrations of the machine doing his job with its metal arm. Emma leans against him, and I eat too much of what they make.

I have accused Paul, who shows up, with or without a bulwark of friends, of trying to run interference between me and Ellis, and I've warned him not to. I won't listen as he details Ellis's losses for me, but I force him to listen as I detail my own back to him. I have begun to work in my studio at night—especially if Paul is here— or more specifically, I retreat, but sit blankly. I don't want to talk to my own friends, because I don't know what I'd say. A few times, I've woken Emma up, only to have her look at me and sleepily ask, "What, Mom?"

During the day I perform a million chores that exhaust me. Yesterday I had to do an emergency floss for Ellis, who had a feather of meat caught in a back molar, but I don't brush his teeth. I don't flush the toilet when he's done unless he comes and asks me to, I don't turn the channel when I see him drooping out of boredom. He's in terrible pain most of the time, worse than before. Ellis has curled his hand protectively against his chest now. The slightest brush against his skin makes him scream, turning even the simplest tasks I do for him into a disaster that leaves me shaking. At night he trembles, sweats, and has nightmares. Yesterday Emma, in a new angora sweater, a present from my mother, walked by her father and the whisper of fur against his knuckles made him pale. When I looked at him, he turned away. We are each other's reminders now.

Tonight, when I'm cooking dinner, Ellis and Emma make an announcement.

"Mom, first you have to sit," Emma instructs.

"I learned how to hold a spoon today," Ellis declares, as though there's an audience in the room. "Actually, *hold* probably isn't the right word. Anyway, Emma here is going to be my lovely assistant."

Emma pulls a large white plastic spoon from under her sweater. It is deep and ladle-like, with a hooked handle. Only Emma is truly patient as she tries to weave the handle through the knot of her father's fingers. Ellis is trying as hard as he can not to show his pain, and he's giving words of encouragement to her, and to himself. I know his love for her will be the singular, immutable fact of her life. The process is so long and excruciating I've got my body in a tight hold to keep myself from screaming. When Ellis grimaces, Emma sees a smile. When his eyes tear and he cries, she hears only a laugh. When he taps his foot under the table, she thinks he's ready to dance with her.

"Great, great—okay, sweetheart, that's enough for now," Ellis tells Emma, who is grinning proudly. I wonder how I can ever take this away from her. Suddenly, Ellis bangs his spooned-fist on the table out of pure frustration, I think, and pretends he is not jolted with agony. But he is too nauseated to eat now, so he sits with his eyes forced wide open, as though he's really having fun, as though he can cast about the pain and distribute it among those he needs to believe really love him. In a few minutes, he asks me to take him upstairs.

In bed, Ellis shivers. Soon the painkillers I've placed on his tongue are going to kick in and he'll be asleep, but in the meantime he can't seem to get warm. His teeth are chattering as I undress and get into bed with him, roll him on his side so I can fit my body around his. I'm thinking of my daughter downstairs, how I've hooked her up once again to the television so I can tend to her father, how she probably understands more than I know. I have a powerful feeling in the dark that mine is not to figure out what shit my husband's left me with, but what I am to do with what I have if I stay. I love Ellis only for what he does for Emma, and that may be enough. At the moment, I want it to be.

"Tell me about the accident," I say. Still, I need specifics, shape, to see it happen. "Just tell me, all right? Don't lie about it or say you don't remember, or tell me something hurts too much. I've pictured you flat on the highway, your arms outstretched, reaching for something—the yellow line?—but I know that can't be, because why would you be doing that? I want to know why it was just your hands and not your legs or your middle cut in half. Where were your hands, Ellis?"

He takes so long to answer I wonder if he's asleep. "The sunroof was open." His voice is surprisingly clear. "The heat was blasting because it was about two degrees out, but the sunroof was open for kicks, and I had my hands sticking out. I was wearing gloves. The car rolled over. She was a little drunk, I guess. The edge of the sunroof is like a Ginsu knife with all that weight and just cut my hand right off. You know how I can be sometimes, Lise. Just crazy, like a kid. It was stupid. It was beyond stupid." He is crying; he's lost his calm, and I know he's terrified. "That's it."

"Not really," I tell him. I hold him tightly, my breasts pressing up against his back. I'm furious at him, hurt more than I can feel, but I'm also taking care of him, warming him. "Tell me some more, I need to know. Did you fuck her first?"

"Oh, Lise," he says, crying now, "yes, you know I did, once, that night. You need me to say I fucked her. Can you believe it doesn't matter at all? I was just having fun. I'm sorry, I was a stupid, happy man."

I don't know if he's right, that I just needed to hear him say it, but I feel some small relief, some familiar threat passing.

One thing about the monkey-wood arch at night is the way it captures and delivers to me in the studio every sound in the house. I have been concentrating on the whine of Emma's snores for a while—she didn't want to go to sleep, cried to stay up, and then immediately peed in her bed—when I hear Ellis get up from the living room where he's been watching a basketball game on television. He makes his familiar way toward me, stops under the arch, and looks at it.

"This is a pretty fine piece of work, you know that?" he says. In the past he has joked about removing the thing and giving it to a museum, or selling it to one of his collectors. Now of course we're really worried about money. "Damn, I was talented." He looks tired and presses his cheek against the wood. "Smells good. I need you to come with me tomorrow, to the hospital. We're trying something new—for the pain."

He's been home for two weeks; now he needs me to go with him. "Fine. I'll come."

"And if it doesn't work, then they'll cut it off," he says, matter-of-factly. He is wearing the same sweatshirt he had on yesterday—my fault. "Dysaesthesia," he explains. "The nerves in my hand are so screwed up they misfire every time I'm touched. Have you noticed? They aren't sending the right message to my brain. Everything that should feel good feels bad."

"I know what you mean." It takes him a second to realize he's supposed to laugh.

I'm a little stunned to find myself back in the hospital, though it feels very familiar. Ellis and I are waiting in one of the activity rooms in the PT clinic. "'Activity,'" Ellis says, staring at the poster of two white-haired people riding bikes, "fat chance."

Martha, his PT, a black woman with closely cropped hair, comes in, nods for Ellis to sit down, and puts a bowl of sand on the table in front of him. She stands with her hands in the pockets of her white coat.

"No thanks, Martha, I'd rather have a jelly donut," Ellis says, leans back, and winks at her. "And a big cup of coffee. So you can take this away."

"Sorry, friend, only sand on this morning's menu." She has barely looked at me—I am just the patient's wife after all—and her attention goes to him. "Desensitization is the word of the day," she tells Ellis, "so do your thing."

The bowl in front of Ellis is ordinary. It may even be Tupperware, cloudy and faintly green, and large enough for a block-party-sized salad, except now it holds sand. Ellis glares at it, but I can't resist touching it, rolling a few hundred grains between my thumb and forefinger.

"Okay, but I'm only going to put my hand in here if you tell me this sand's from Aruba and once upon a time had ten lovely women lying on it," Ellis offers, a little sadly. Even he knows he's lost his charm.

"It had ten naked fat boys lying in it," Martha says, her face very serious. Ellis shrugs and then moves his two-fingered hand toward the bowl but doesn't take it any farther. I can tell that Martha likes Ellis—they've had their laughs together these weeks, but that's not going to happen today. "Now stick that hand of yours in there because I have other things to do besides baby-sit you," she says, and leaves the room.

Ellis looks up at me. "No big deal, right? Just a bowl of sand."

"Just a bowl of sand," I say. We both know there's an urgency here. "Touch a few grains first. Like this." I pick up a pinchful and rain it back onto the bowl.

"You think that's so great?" Ellis yells with mock challenge. "Watch this."

He lowers his hand toward the bowl again, and this time his fingers actually touch the surface. I can see each grain rolling under the pressure. "No fucking problem," he says, as he pushes deeper. Suddenly, I see that an odd muscle at the base of his chin has stiffened, and his legs shoot straight out under the table. Still, he's digging deeper, biting his lip, and I'm holding my breath.

Ellis lets out a shriek that brings Martha running, wiping her hands on her white coat. She's just in time to see him jerk his hand out of the bowl and start waving it around as though it's on fire. I'm amazed at how it seems to rotate on the bone. Sand flies through the room, pecking away at my face. Martha stands shielded by the door, and Ellis screams so loudly that the only pain I'm sure he can feel anymore is in his throat.

"Oh boy," Martha says, and shakes her head when Ellis is finally quiet. She explains to me now, as my husband struggles to catch his breath, that the objective is to overload Ellis with sensory stimulus so that eventually he won't be able to feel anything, good or bad. It is a concept that turns my stomach. "And you didn't do so good," she informs him.

"No shit," he says, angrily.

We're given a break to have some coffee, a cup of water, and though I'm deeply dreading it, Ellis wants to try the sand again. I can't sit still, so I pace the room and remind Ellis that as an incentive Paul and a group of friends are taking him out for a beer tonight. Ellis is concentrating on the bowl of sand in front of him, but not moving toward it. I know, and he knows, that today will be the last time he'll be able to do this, if he can actually do it at all. The first time around, the mind allows itself to forget; pain was an aberration, a mismemory, it says, so be hopeful. But the second time around, pain becomes a fact you can't forget.

And I can't watch, so I leave Ellis alone in the room and enter the larger open space of physical therapy where people are performing various simple tasks: leg lifts, head tilts, deep breaths. The room stinks of mentholated rub, and I'm thinking of a time when Emma was home sick and Ellis and I took turns rubbing her chest.

When Ellis's wail has peaked and finally ebbed—and how come no one else seems struck enough by the misery of it to look up?—I go back into the room to find the bowl overturned and the sand cascading to the floor. There is sand in his beard and his hair, on his shirt, stuck to his lips. Disease loves disorder, and he's going to lose this hand too. Distantly, I wonder when it will be my turn to recuperate from this. Ellis is retching now, his head between his knees, and so I sit down with him and put my hand on his back. It's almost time to pick up Emma at school, I remind him; we don't want her to be the last one left on the curb.

When my son Lee lost another job, he came home again. After two and a half years in Florida, his skin had taken on a salutary glow, and as I watched him one morning move through an autumn's low-lying overcast, his color alone seemed a warning to me, a red beam approaching in the fog. Out in the wide expanse of driveway behind our angled Victorian, Lee rode my rusted bike which he'd found earlier among the tall boxwoods.

In the carriage house that my wife and I had converted for our catering business, I waited for Lee to put the bike away and come to work. He sang with a hard-mouthed concentration, his tone rising and falling as the circles he made closed and widened in some precise geometry stored in his head. One of the airless tires slapped against the gravel like a disapproving tongue. Though it was mid-October and now had begun to rain, my son's feet were bare on the chalky black pedals, and he was wearing only jeans and a T-shirt from Drain, a downtown club he'd been in very late the night before. Hungover, he now seemed to be undizzying himself.

Across the driveway, Anna stood at the back door of our house and watched Lee too. Earlier, I'd seen her get dressed to meet prospective clients—a bride and her mother—and she'd looked beautiful in a rose silk dress and earrings that dangled like silver droplets. In the last two years she had thrown herself into this part of the business—the part I didn't like—with great success. People detected in Anna an unspoken sympathy; they saw a woman who understood it's okay to go a little crazy over the details.

Anna and I had turned fifty the year before, and while she teased herself about the new lines that radiated from the corners of her eyes, I only noticed how her mouth had grown fuller, her eyes clearer. The years with Lee gone in Florida had softened Anna, and her expressions, expectations, and pleasures sometimes appeared as easily as full blooms. Now, even through glass, I saw a net of tension cast over her face once again, one of the casualties my son's return had already laid out.

If I squinted at Lee in the driveway, I could see him as others might: a twenty-four-year-old man with a handsome, complicated face and a powerful presence despite the fact that he was riding in sloping circles. But if I gave my son a full assessing stare, as Anna did, I couldn't see him as anything other than my fuckup of a boy, my confused, impulsive, challenging child. Of all the terms we'd heard over the years, challenging was the one I hated most, as if Lee were a mountain to move or a set of encyclopedias to memorize; all I needed to do was apply myself.

Lee stopped riding when Anna locked the back door and walked to her car. He put out his hand, but she brushed by, as though he were merely an errant tree branch or a stranger. Lee asked his mother where she was going, when she'd be back. He sensed her irritation with him—for staying out so late, for oversleeping, for making me wait, maybe for simply being back again—and his voice was tinged with a child's willingness to try his luck with her.

Anna didn't answer Lee, but did turn to see where he was, so she wouldn't hit him as she backed out her Toyota. My son's face deflated at his failure to engage her, and then in a quick switch he pretended she'd run over his feet. He danced around with a terrible, wolfish howl, his head thrown back, his mouth wide open. I felt the neighborhood shudder at his return.

Anna stopped the car to consider the likelihood of having hurt him. I had moved up to the sliding glass door by then and she looked at me. Lee hasn't changed, she'd said to me days earlier, and neither have you with your ready excuses for him. Anna had not fought Lee's return—it was one of our unspoken agreements that he could always come back—but she seemed used up this time, by both memory and foreboding. She backed the rest of the way down the driveway, her face set with purpose.

Anna and I visited Lee in Florida only once. His brother was going to join us—we'd counted on Peter's normalizing effects—but he'd changed his mind at the last minute. Standing in the Jacksonville airport, I don't know if it was a sudden whoosh of humidity or the sight of Lee loping toward us in a pair of purple flip-flops that made me go weak with misgiving and protective love. I had learned over the years that if I allowed myself to picture him out in the world I became distracted with worry, so I forced myself not to picture him at all. Here he was, smiling against a backdrop of palm trees and overweight travelers, talking to us before we could even hear what he was saying.

He'd brought a single rose for his mother and presented it to her with a lover's kneel. Anna, embarrassed, tried to pull him up off the gum-spotted carpet. Lee had roped his girlfriend into picking us up. On the drive to the resort hotel where they both worked, Lee pointed out the roadside swamps that he swore harbored alligators. He kept his fingers on his girlfriend's sinewy neck. I held Anna's hand.

Lee was a waiter at Courtside, the hotel's sports restaurant that overlooked the tennis courts and golf course beyond. When we'd wanted to reach him, we'd had to call the number at the bar, and on that first afternoon I began to place the noises that had accompanied our talks: the melancholy gulp of tennis ball machines, voices slipping out between swings of the fake-frontier doors. Lee yanked people by the arm to come meet us; these were the friends we'd been hearing about.

Lee lived in a dark, tilting shack owned by the hotel, close to Courtside but hidden behind lichen-colored wisps of Spanish moss. It was hard for me to look at the place and not feel he'd unwittingly stepped into some darker time. But back in our large ocean-front room, Anna said how happy Lee seemed to be. For a second, the word surprised her, but it pleased her too. She said Lee had finally found a contained world for himself, and fewer options meant fewer bad choices.

Anna was able to step back for the full view when she talked about Lee, but I wasn't, and I'd thought then of his room above our carriage house, his work in the business, all of it also a contained life within our citified half-acre. Too contained? I didn't know. The last time Lee had lived and worked with us—and the times before—he'd tested us, disappointed us, and pushed impossibly hard until we asked him to leave. I would have let it go on—Lee was on a cycle's downswing, and he'd lift again—but Anna couldn't.

Like investors who believe troubling times are finally behind them, we left Florida and went home to Providence and hired a girl named Renee to take Lee's place in the business. Seven months later, when he came back to us without explanation, I recalled how much I'd hated the feel of the Spanish moss as I swept it away from my face to get to Lee's shack. He had watched, absorbed by the movements of attachment, as I removed a sticky veil of it from his mother's hair. I couldn't help thinking that our visit had done the same thing somehow, swept moss away from an idea better left in the dark, one that nudged at him to return home again.

Now I opened the sliding glass door and yelled at Lee to come inside.

"What's wrong with Mom?" he asked, and let the bike tip to the gravel.

Distantly, I heard the rumble of the exhaust-snorting car driven by Renee's father which brought her to work in the mornings and picked her up at the end of each day.

"Nothing. She was in a hurry."

Mornings, after Lee's return, when it was just the two of us in the carriage house—Anna out on a client call—I'd work next to my son at the wooden island, relaxed in our friendship and conversation. Our knives chopped at companionable odds, and our shoulders touched. I'd watch Lee place a tiny candy rose on a chocolate cookie, or slice strawberries so thin they appeared like parted lips, and I'd allow myself to feel this balance I'd constructed could hold forever.

I loved my business and was good at it. I could do without the unpredictability of spoilage and the way food acted like a barometer for all sorts of weather. I could do without clients who whined or held onto my bills like toothpicks after they'd gulped down the boiled shrimp, but I never once regretted changing careers. It was a great thrill to have found out, as I edged into middle age, that there were some surprises left in me, that I was able to do something I'd never imagined I could.

It had been ten years since I'd left the law firm of Landau & Skoyles, but I could still recall the unaccountable flickers of panic that sometimes seized me in the lull of a meeting or the loneliness of a late night at my desk. There were periods I was so consumed by the work that I had little idea of what was happening with my family. But finally it was the look of strained patience on Anna's face when I'd come home in the evening, and Peter in his spotless room, that hit me hardest in the chest. Lee's day of energy and drama had finished them both off. He'd have some left, though, so I put him to the task of making dinner with me. As Lee served his mother and brother with great pride and contentment, I saw something of myself in him.

When I made up my mind to quit the firm, I took Ted Landau out for a drink to explain myself. I'm leaving to help with my son,

I said. He has some behavioral problems, he's impulsive, needs attention. Anna's exhausted, and I want to do my share. It pained me to have to listen to Landau tell me how admirable it all was when I knew he really wondered what kind of man I'd let myself become. But if I'd left my career for Lee, I also knew I was doing it to save myself.

Soon, instead of Anna, I was the one trying to defuse various situations with Lee. Once, at school, he decided to amuse his study-hall classmates by banging his head against the wall. He didn't stop until he had everyone howling, dots of blood had appeared on his forehead, and a panicked substitute teacher had run for help. Another time, I hurried to collect him from a friend's house where "things" had gotten too wild, I was told by a tight-lipped mother. I carted a sullen boy to the shrink's and, sitting in the outer office, strained to hear what was being said. (Was it something Anna and I had done? I wanted to know. And when had it all started?) I doled out pills and monitored side effects— dry mouth and drowsiness, elation and cheeks that looked as though they'd been slapped. Half the kids I hear about today remind me of Lee back then.

When the business took hold, I created a space for it in the carriage house. The next year—the year Peter couldn't get off to college fast enough—I made a bedroom above for Lee, who was spending less time at school and more with me. The work area was high-ceilinged and light, its concrete floor painted a soothing sea-green. Lee's room was like a nest, low-eaved, honey-brown, and smelled of clean wood. Working side by side every day, my son siphoned love from me. I have enough—and for Anna too, I told myself—if we just stay *exactly* like this.

"If you want to be my lover," Lee sang, in a pinched falsetto to the whine of music that leaked from Renee's headphones. Side by side at the work counter, he was tall and broad; she was half his size. Lee bumped her hips with his, and she bumped back.

"Crank it up," he yelled to her. "I love this song."

Renee turned a falsely impatient profile to him, the tip of her thin nose almost luminescent in the light.

"No way. I'll blow my eardrums out," she said, unaware of how loudly she was speaking. Protectively, she patted her Walkman, which was the color of a police caution tape.

Lee lifted the delicate pad of Renee's headphones from her ear. She looked up at him expectantly—he had been home for five weeks and was still something of a mystery to her—as he rounded toward her to whisper.

"Okay," he shouted instead, his voice a bark which snapped above our heads.

Renee was startled, and I waited to see what she would do next. At eighteen, it seemed, any attention from a man was still attention, and she blushed. When she saw me watching, she went back to slicing vegetables. Renee worked with surprising skill, given her fingers, which were as narrow and delicate as candles. She had thin, colorless hair pulled back in a gather of cloth, and eyes so unremarkable you might assume she thought of nothing all day long. She gave no sign she understood directions when I gave them to her but always did what I asked. Even as I'd interviewed her for the job, and tried to coax from her more than a single-word response, I'd have bet she wouldn't last with us for very long. I hired her anyway. As Renee glanced again at Lee, I thought of her father, an abrupt, impatient man, suspicious of me in our few conversations, as though pâtés and stuffed mushrooms—as though *I*—were a front for something else.

Lee continued to sing to her music and create a mosaic of cheese on a glass platter. When he was little, Anna used to tell me that if she held his hand or hovered inches from it when he drew, he created fanciful whirls and radiating patterns. But the minute he sensed his mother's lessening of attention his pencil wandered off the paper like a drunk off a curb.

Anna sat at her desk and watched as paper began to spit out of her printer and shimmy to the floor. "I have no idea what's wrong with this thing," she said to no one in particular. "I asked it to print out two copies, but I guess it didn't believe me. It's hard not to think these machines have sadistic minds of their own."

"Let me look at it for you," Lee offered. He wiped his hands down the front of his pants. "I can probably fix it too. I'm good with computers because no one else in the restaurant has any clue."

"I don't think so, Lee," she said. "You need to finish what you're doing. Don't you have to make an eleven-thirty delivery, Davis?" It was a nudge for me, but for Lee to hear; he had already made us late the week before.

"Eleven-thirty, " I said. "At the very latest."

"Plenty of time," Lee drawled in some strange accent, "plenty of time. Mother should not worry about son. Mother should trust son, be cool about son. Son is not total fuckup, won't break computer, won't mess up big, important job."

In the past, Anna might have argued with Lee, but now she retreated into the forest of pictures she'd crowded her desk with. There was a picture of Peter and his fiancee that I'd never seen before. I knew I hadn't given my oldest son nearly enough—need takes different shapes—and it hurt me to think about.

"Mother should let son help," Lee went on. "Be nice to son."

"Stop it," I said, and then, to distract him from his tense focus on Anna, I added, "That plate looks good, so finish it up now." I touched him on the shoulder and felt how tight he was, how in the space of a few minutes he'd gone from singing to anger. "Let's just wrap this up, okay? Renee, you almost done?" She gave me her usual shrug.

"I think this looks like crap, actually," Lee said. He stared at the platter of cheese in disgust, as though he'd had nothing to do with it. With an abrupt slap of his hand, he flipped the plate over on the counter, scattering the food everywhere. "I'm going to try something else."

"We don't have all that much time," I told him.

"I'll go fast. You're the one who said it should look good for the job."

"What matters is that you get it done, that you follow through. You know the routine, we've been making this same delivery for weeks, for years. Just finish it up. It's a goddamn plate of cheese, Lee."

In fact the job, which ran from July until late November, had been a major account for us for years, a series of weekly catered lunches for Landau & Skoyles that led to much of our other work. Lee knew I disliked this particular job—I revealed too much to him sometimes—going back to my old offices, serving food I knew most of the lawyers would be too busy to eat or appreciate. Still, it was evidence of my confidence, and in the decisions I'd made, and I wouldn't give it up. Sometimes my attention to detail—the scalloped radishes and abundant salads—were a bitter touch on those occasions, but I reminded myself how lucky I was to be doing what I loved.

"You don't even like those assholes," Lee reminded me. "You shouldn't worry about what they're going to think."

Renee, tongue poised on a worried upper lip, watched. "I'll just do it," she announced, and moved between us.

"I have a better idea," I said, unnerved. "You two go take a break, walk around the yard or something. Work it off, Lee," I opened the door for them and took a great gulp of the cool air as they left.

I turned back to the counter and hastily rearranged the cheese, which was beginning to shrink from too much touching. It gave off a warm, breathy smell. Outside, Lee patiently tossed a Frisbee to Renee which she was unable to catch.

"He's really an optimist, isn't he?" Anna said as she watched. She'd come to stand next to me and put her hands on the counter.

"Lee only wants to engage you, Anna, get your attention," I told her. "Your indifference infuriates him. I don't see the point."

"I'm not indifferent at all." She sighed, as though she'd come to this reluctantly, but firmly. "I'm just done. I don't know what to do with him now—it's the same story over and over again." Out in the yard, inches from Lee, Renee bent over to wipe away the flecks of grass from her white sneakers. He looked over her arched back at us and raised his eyebrows. Anna rested her fingertips on her cheek. "He hasn't changed, not in all the time he was gone, and he's not going to now."

If I'd suspected it since Lee's return, I now knew Anna was the one who had changed. She had allowed herself not to see Lee as her future anymore.

When we drove downtown to Landau & Skoyles a few hours later, for the first time I let Lee and Renee take the food to the tenth floor alone. Anna had thrown it all to me now—she'd made that clear—and I told myself Lee could handle more responsibility if given the chance, he'd grow into it. He might even thrive—and wasn't this what I'd been hoping for for years? I'd gone over and over the setting up and serving, the collecting and cleaning routine with him. Renee's solemn nod—she and I had been doing this together for months—reassured me it would be fine.

From the van, I watched the two of them walk through the revolving glass door, holding trays of food aloft. Lee had changed his clothes, but I didn't realize until he'd gone around in the door three times pretending he couldn't stop that he was wearing the chambray shirt I often wore on jobs. Lee might have reached into my closet for the shirt, but I preferred to think Anna had given it to him.

A week later, Anna and I worked in the carriage house. It was a wet afternoon, and I considered turning on the lights, but I was hesitant to scatter a duskiness that had settled between us. Lee and Renee had delivered another lunch to the law firm without me that morning, and all of us had spent the rest of the day cleaning and reorganizing. Renee's father had been over an hour late picking her up, and the room still had a stench of exhaust, a graceless smell I'd begun to associate with her coming and going. She had stood miserably by the door waiting, her raincoat squeaking like a box of mice when she sighed.

I'd once admitted to Lee—and heard the hint of caution in my voice—that I felt a little sorry for Renee, how her life was so narrow I couldn't imagine a future that would be much different. And I knew Lee had been thinking of this when he offered to drive Renee home and tried to comfort her, painfully flip-flopping between assurances and nasty comments about her father. Anna had blamed the weather.

Now I looked over at my wife, and despite the shadows, still took comfort in the simple fact of her familiarity, her place. But if I'd hoped for some glimmer of connection in return, it wasn't there. Instead, Anna watched the rain that pelted the driveway and filled the room with the gloominess of things I was suddenly afraid I'd lost and might not be able to get back.

When the phone rang, Anna answered it. I hadn't noticed just how dark the room had become until I saw her face inches from the silver computer screen, as though she needed light to listen. She said a few soft words. When she hung up, I turned on the fluorescent light above the work counter and my eyes contracted painfully.

"That was Ted Landau," Anna said. "First he wanted to let us know how good the lunches have been this year. Then he said some crystal thing is missing from the office."

"Crystal thing," I repeated. "What does that mean?"

Anna pushed away from the desk and her feet fell flat against the concrete floor. "Well, apparently, one of the attorneys had a paperweight, a glass obelisk, on her desk for some award she'd won, and now it's gone. Ted found it necessary to apologize for all the silly things women feel compelled to keep on their desks. Was he always such a prick?"

Anna began to order her desk and close it down for the night.

"And?" My hands were suddenly cold.

"And he thought we might keep an eye out for the thing."

"That's it?" I asked. "Keep an eye out for the thing like it's going to walk up the driveway one morning? He thinks Lee took it, doesn't he?"

"He didn't say that, Davis. He said they're looking into all the possibilities—the cleaners, the delivery people. Probably even their clients. People are in and out of there all the time. You know what it's like."

"But tell me what you really think."

She hesitated, and then turned to keep her concern hidden, "I think if it were me, if I worked there, I wouldn't leave anything out in the open. I'm going home."

I changed my clothes and went to the high school track for a run. The rain had stopped by then, and the smell of wet cinders stung my sinuses, like the pressure just before a nosebleed. Soon, the lights around the track burned on and revealed a group of kids in the misty center, kicking around a giant orange Gatorade barrel. Bored and uninspired, they looked like trouble, but didn't all kids? Like them, Lee had probably scared plain men like me with his reckless gestures and hurled remarks, but what, finally, I was furious to know, had he ever done to *hurt* anyone? Lee was so much pain, a threat to my marriage, a million years of worry— and now this too—but I wanted him with me.

That night I said nothing to Lee about the obelisk. It wasn't just that I was afraid he had lifted some shiny hunk of glass that caught his eye the second I stopped watching him. It was out of some larger fear of discovering he had finally wandered beyond the protective walls I'd set up for him.

One evening when Anna and I were eating an almost silent dinner, Landau called to let me know the obelisk had still not turned up. Even as he talked, I saw lights on in Lee's room above the carriage house and knew I'd have to go there. Anna glanced down at her plate when I told her.

An indirect accusation is worse than one that comes head-on; you have an entire lifetime of guilt, missteps, and evidence to sift through, and as I walked across the driveway, I remembered a time Lee, at nine, had arranged a birthday party for his mother. He'd led us down the street to the Italo Restaurant, and at the table gave Anna a heart-shaped pin that he'd wrapped in a paper towel. For a confusing moment, she didn't say anything, but stared at the pin in her hand. When she looked up, her mouth was tight in surprise, but her eyes were full of sorrow, as though she'd just heard terrible news. She turned to Lee, who was dragging on a breadstick the way I was dragging on my cigarette, and asked him where he'd gotten the pin. Lee went goofy because he knew it made her laugh, and then quickly admitted he'd taken the pin from his grandmother's jewelry box. She had four of them, so it wasn't really stealing, he said; he only wanted her to have one too.

At the carriage house, I found that Lee had left the door unlocked though he'd been told not to. The ground floor was dark, but upstairs the shower was running. I hadn't been in Lee's room since the day he moved back and I'd helped him carry his two duffel bags in from the car. The room had a cheesy smell of unwashed clothes and dirty bedsheets. Day-glo posters, unfurled after years in a closet, had been tacked to the sloping walls. I wished we'd thrown them out. On the table by the window were the remains of a sandwich, and Renee's Walkman, its bright yellow box and delicate headphones unmistakable. Lee was singing in the shower, the same tune over and over. An old television with bent aerials was propped on an empty milk crate at the foot of the bed next to the window. And sitting on top was the crystal obelisk.

Lee didn't notice me when he came out of the bathroom without anything on. It was just like him to stand in front of an open window and air-dry himself. I hadn't seen my son naked in years. He was stunning, a series of balanced geometries made more compelling by his unself-consciousness. Where have you fallen from? I wanted to ask.

He swore when he saw me. His penis was tumescent with that odd, pleading angle of a dog lifting its sleepy head. Of course he'd been masturbating in the shower, and why not? I thought bitterly. I pushed him, my hands slipping on his wet shoulders. Lee had never backed away from a fight in his life, but he stopped himself now because I was his father and not as strong as he was, and I thought, finally, with the unreasonable relief that comes in the worst times, the boy has some sense.

I backed him hard up against the wall. His skull smacked one of the low beams.

"What is that?" I demanded, and nodded toward the obelisk.

"What?" Lee said. He rubbed his head.

"That glass thing."

"A trophy." Lee tried to shrug me off.

"Where did you get it, you little shit?"

"Come on, Dad, get off me," he said, and I stepped back. I remembered how quickly Peter had always let his hands drop from Lee—now I heard the tone of warning myself. Lee pulled on a pair of pants, shaking his feet through the legs. "What's the problem?"

"You better tell me where you got it."

"Around." His hands slipped into his pockets. "Okay, from the law firm. In one of the offices."

Why had Lee never learned to lie? Always fess up, I'd taught him. Now my piousness came back at me with an ugly force.

Lee ran a finger up the obelisk's sharp edge. "Renee said it was the prettiest thing she's ever seen, and she has nothing. I was going to give it to her, but she said her father would go bullshit, so I kept it here. It's not much, kind of ugly, but she visits it, holds it up to the light and looks through it."

"You took it for Renee? You're just a saint, aren't you, Lee?"

I punched my son deep in the stomach. It wasn't as hard as I could have hit, but hard enough to make him bark for breath. Hard enough for a filament of spit to hang from his mouth like a silver string, pulling him down until he fell to his knees. I'd never hurt him before, and it was hard enough that he would never do this to us again.

I went to see Landau very early the next morning. I carried the obelisk in a plastic bag and as I went through the revolving door it hit the metal frame. From its off-key ring, I knew I'd chipped it.

At the bottom of the bag, I found a tiny half-moon the size of a child's fingernail and I slipped it into my pocket.

"Okay," Landau nodded as I placed the obelisk on a far table. He didn't get up to inspect it, but leaned so far back in his leather chair I considered finishing the job and pushing him though the window. He waited for me to offer humility and an explanation. The plastic bag hung limp in my hand.

"Let's get Ms. Lewison in here, see if we can resolve this," he said and gazed down at something on his desk as he spoke to his secretary.

I'd never really looked closely at Landau since I left the firm, but now I did. I'd heard his wife was sick, a grandchild was blind; he seemed dissipated and a little frayed, like his surroundings. When Ms. Lewison came in, Landau pointed to her obelisk. "I've known Davis forever," he told her. "We used to work together, as a matter of fact, in the firm's younger days. And Anna, his wife, terrific woman. Admirable people, both of them." And he knew our son too, he'd talked to him just a few weeks ago. The boy had some emotional difficulties, behavioral problems, he was why I'd left the firm years ago, and now he was back living and working with us. Wasn't that right? he asked me.

The woman gave me a look of pity. I fingered the glass chip in my pocket and felt it razor away at the callused tip of my finger.

"It wasn't my son," I said. To give up Lee now was unbearable. "There's a girl working for us—*was* working for us. She has a lot of problems, bad family situation, I'm sure I don't know the half of it. It was a risk hiring her, but we thought we'd give her a chance."

Landau whistled through his teeth. "You're good, Davis. You always do the things the rest of us are much too afraid of." He turned toward the other lawyer. "This sounds reasonable."

She agreed it did, picked up the obelisk, and left the room. If she discovered it was chipped, it would be too late. Landau wouldn't go any further with it.

"Too bad about that girl," Landau said when it was my turn

to be ushered out. His voice was cloying next to my ear, his hand on my shoulder. "I had a nice conversation with her the other day when she was up here. Shy, but on the ball, doing a good job. Jesus, people *are* unpredictable, aren't they? We'll see you next week."

From a pay phone in the glaring marble lobby, I called Renee. The metal booth stank of cigarettes and piss.

"Hullo?" she answered. A baby cried in the background.

"It's me, Davis." I paused. "You were probably getting ready to come to work."

"Uh huh. My dad's going to drive me."

With Lee home now, I explained, the words as slippery in my mouth as nausea, we couldn't keep her on anymore. I was really very, very sorry, she'd been wonderful, a great worker, and I would send her two months' pay, and maybe sometime later if we needed her again . . . I thanked her for everything once more, and when she didn't respond, I hung up.

I sat down on a bench in the center of the lobby. Thin music flowed from somewhere. I thought about Renee and remembered a day months before Lee returned, when just the two of us were in the carriage house. She'd been unusually lighthearted, and in a rare moment her hands sent a ceramic plate off the counter and smashing to the floor. She ran into the bathroom and slammed the door. I could hear her crying, and after a few minutes I knocked, opened the door, and told her to come out. She wouldn't move from the tight corner where she was wedged, so I went in.

"It's okay," I said, and when I put my arms around her, she stiffened. "Don't be upset. We were having some fun, and these things happen. We'll clean it up, start again. Come on, Renee, I'm not going to fire you."

At home, I told Anna things with Landau had gone fine and were settled, and for the moment it seemed that was all she wanted to hear. In the carriage house, I watched her try to decide whether or not to ask Lee to move from her desk. She approached, she backed off. Lee wouldn't look at either of us in his posed preoccupation. Anna was going to meet clients, but finally, instead of leaving, she lugged the bucket of birdseed out into the yard, only to discover that Lee had already refilled the feeder. For a few minutes she stared down the driveway, then knocked on the glass to wave me outside with her.

"Renee's late," she said. "I wonder if something's happened. She hasn't called."

Anna shivered in the cold without her coat. I might have put my arm around her then, but I looked at my watch instead and tried to focus in on some sense of time. The day was forming into sharp, unconnected bursts.

"Maybe her father just decided not to drive her here anymore," Anna said. She picked up the bucket of seed and let it bump against her leg, rocking her a little. "Very possible. He's a strange man."

I told Anna that it was Renee who had stolen the obelisk I'd found in Lee's room, and of course I'd had to fire her for it. My wife nodded—her body drooped a little in relief—and when she went inside to get her things, stopped to talk to Lee. She stroked his head when she said good-bye.

That night in bed, Anna was roused first by a distant rumble. Maybe Lee being dropped off, she muttered to comfort herself. In her sleep, even past midnight, her maternal worry leaked out. When we awoke again, more of a shot to the back of the neck this time, I recognized the roar and throb of the car that sat in our driveway.

"What is it?" Anna sat up. She was naked, her body rubbed soft by sleep.

"Nothing. It's fine, it's not near. Go back to sleep."

But Anna went to the window, and I felt the warmth of our bed skitter away. "Renee's father," she said. "He's here."

I stood next to Anna and watched the man get out of his car. Renee was motionless in the front seat.

"Are you going down?" Anna asked.

"No."

Renee's father paced in the driveway, his legs bisected by headlights. He circled the van, then pulled at the door of the carriage house that I hoped Lee had locked for once. I could make out a very faint green glow inside from the clock above the stove, but the rest was a dense black. If Lee was home at all, his room was still dark. Renee's father gestured to his daughter, and she leaned on the horn. Then he opened her door and waved Renee out so that she stood in the headlights. He called my name.

"I think you should go talk to him," Anna said.

"What are you sending me into?" I turned to her. "Look at him, Anna. The guy's crazy."

"My daughter is a good girl," Renee's father yelled, his voice carrying on a channel of air that led right to us. "She doesn't need shit like this, people telling lies and saying she stole when she didn't. Your son—he's the thief."

I backed up and sat on the bed. "He's crazy," I said again. "He doesn't know what he's talking about."

"Davis. This morning I told Lee that you fired Renee for stealing the paperweight and he told me the truth. He said you knew it. Lee must have let Renee know what happened."

And then suddenly I lifted and thought, but Anna doesn't get how Lee has made up for everything now by going to Renee, by owning up. There is something good in him too, I had to tell her, and he has righted this for all of us.

"You gave Renee up like she was nothing." Anna spoke first, and her voice rose. "As if she didn't matter. What a hateful thing you've done. What's *happened* to you, Davis?"

"What was I supposed to do?"

"Tell the truth."

"What good would that do?" I stood again and looked out the window. Renee's father was still yelling as he got into his car. "I did this for all of us. There was no choice. *This* is our life."

"But your lying for Lee has no place here," she said. "He has to go."

"What's the point, Anna? He'll just be back, we'll do all of this again. You know that."

"No, *you* have to tell him he can't come back, ever. We're done now, Davis. This finally has to stop."

The next morning I went to the carriage house, but sat down on the stairs before I went up to Lee's room. Anna and I had always sent him away when we couldn't live with him anymore, and when he needed to come home, we took him back. It was this push and pull of parenthood that made me recall the easy summers we spent in a house on Slough Pond when the kids were young. I was still working as a lawyer, and we had not yet begun to sort through what was pathology and what was personality with Lee. Three-quarters around the small pond, a sluiceway connected our pond to another. The sluiceway was an hourglass of white sand, very shallow, five feet wide at most, and the gentlest massage of water flowed back and forth through it.

I taught the boys to swim there, slowly testing the widening distances. On the day I encouraged Lee to swim through the sluiceway, when all good things were still possible, I found him sitting at the pinched waist between the two ponds. I asked him what he was doing, leaning over like that, his hands trying to catch the water as it flowed by. He was young then, only eight, and thought he could stop one pond from emptying into the other.

Finally, I stood and went upstairs where Lee was asleep. He was still in the clothes he'd worn the day before, and I wondered if he already knew what I was going to tell him. Dressed, he could always assure himself he'd just stopped by, he hadn't meant to stay for very long anyway. I leaned over him, and his face, so unguarded in sleep, was not completely familiar to me. When I woke him, I said the words, that he had to go and couldn't come back, but I didn't mean them. I didn't even believe them.

This morning, I didn't shovel away last night's snow, and now Bernard is muttering things like "Damn" and "A man could kill himself on this." He can be short with me sometimes, and still wants his house kept up (though he doesn't always notice when I let something go, or leave the dishes for a day), and reminds me often enough of *his* work credo, "Attend to All Things."

If he had the chance, his son Cam would remind me too, speaking through narrow lips and a mouth that opens only a sliver, as though he's trapped something horrible inside. He'd say that shoveling is part of my job, and here's proof that I can't do what I'm paid for, but he doesn't know the half of it. What about loving Bernard with a true heart? I'd ask him. Am I paid for that too? Tell me, Bernard's damp-as-gray-sand son, how much is *that* worth? You shovel the snow yourself. You feel how cold life can be.

We're almost at my car now. Bernard moves through the snow without lifting his feet, so that it begins to pile up on the toes of the Tote's rubbers I bought for him last week. Today he looks like a goblin, tiny and white-haired, his head bent, making two long tracks in the snow. His gloves are big and his fingers droop. The car is only fifteen feet away at most, but he stops.

"I'm slipping, Lila," he says. His voice is half-hidden by the scarf around his neck and a gurgle of phlegm.

"What are you talking about? You're not even moving."

"Yes I am. Watch." And before I know it, he inches ahead of me, and his feet slide out from beneath him. I catch Bernard under the arms, and his hat scratches my chin. My heart is thumping, but I can feel how calm he is and how light. Children grow when they sleep, but old people evaporate at night, they float toward the ceiling in little wisps, and every day there's a little less of Bernard.

"See?" he says—his voice has a snap to it—"you have to take better care of me, Lila," and he walks ahead. That's Bernard, at eighty-four, still with the perfect setup, always a test to see if I'm really there and watching all the time, because one thing he hates is not being watched. Love has made him needy. Bernard is quiet while I warm up the car, and he must be wondering why we're taking my banged-up Escort when we always take his Buick. The seats in his car have a nap you can run your fingers through; the vinyl seats in mine are brittle with cold, cracked from heat. A clear drop hangs from the end of Bernard's veined nose. Any other day, I would have wiped it away, but this morning I don't.

"They haven't plowed the streets yet," Bernard says. He'd tell me about the failings of city services on a normal day, but now he seems concerned with the curtain of snow that's fallen across the windshield. He has the mayor's phone number in his Rolodex, a direct line to the presidents of companies, and he expects things to be taken care of. "Where are we going?"

"Did you forget already?" I say, though I never told him where we're headed, because the truth is, I don't know yet. He's content to think this is just another one of our drives we've been taking more and more of lately, another day we're going to explore without a map, even in this stinging weather. Last Sunday we drove to Massachusetts until the road curled into itself like a fist and stopped at a place called Lands End. Bernard insisted that the ocean was on the other side of the rocks and graph of bare trees, and so we climbed and huffed and stood paralyzed for a few min-utes in the terrible cold, sniffed the spray of the waves, and drove home again. After each of these adventures, he thanks me, and says there's so much out there he doesn't know about, so much he wants to see.

And then, as though to balance out this confession, he boasts of a success thirty years ago, or talks again about his award from the Chamber of Commerce. It strikes me now that these trips have been preparation for the day—this day, maybe—when we don't turn around at Lands End or Provincetown, or the scalloped edge of Newport, but keep on going.

Bernard's head rocks back and forth as we leave Providence. Hope Street is deserted this early, and as I run red lights, clods of snow explode under my tires. I hear it now; the sound is what longing and escape are made of.

An old man can sleep anywhere, anytime, and Bernard slides into a nap. The gloves lie at his feet, soaking up the snow on the floor. There's a fluttering at his fingertips, and his eyes are still open the tiniest, glossiest bit even though he's asleep and snoring. You might think it's mistrust, but I know it isn't. Someday, on that last day I guess, I'll close his silver eyelids for him, like the paper blinds on a dollhouse window, my fingertips ever so light so as not to tear anything.

I was invisible the night I met Bernard over a year ago, a nonvi-sion in all-beige, a woman melting into the carpets, the walls, the faces of people I didn't want to know, at a party where I didn't want to be in the first place. I had lots of good reasons for feeling like a perfect nobody that night (and many, many before it); at forty-one, my life was not what it was meant to be, but most of all, I had a heart, and it was untouched, all pretty and wrapped up in an unopened package.

I was thinking of ditching the friend who'd dragged me along to the Jacobs Plastic holiday party. My mother used to open the door when my father smoked in the house, and I thought that's how I'd like to disappear, sucked out into cold air. An old man had stationed himself in front of the "What's New in Molded Materials" display. No one went over there to look at the Band-Aid-colored drink tumblers and tropical picnic plates in the glass case; they went to be with him. It wasn't that the guy was stunning to look at—there's the flaky, scabby truth of old age—or loud enough to catch your attention. I knew by the way he talked and stroked his mustache, picked up a stuffed-something being passed to him and sniffed it before he took a bite, that he'd always been at the center of things. I know nothing about planets, but he made me think of the sun.

He had that light some people have from the minute they're born, a glow the rest of us want to lean into, and so I moved toward him. Others referred to him as Mr. Jacobs, but the man, fortyish, who was rocking on the balls of his feet just behind, called him Father and tried to talk over him. After a while, I willed myself to say something about work—that was the topic of conversation—and slowly, because Bernard has never been one to admit you've caught his eye, he turned to me.

"And what do you do?" he asked.

We talked for a few minutes and I told him how unhappy I was with my job. He said he was looking for an assistant. His son, still bouncing, straining a bit, tried to break into the circle that now contained me and Bernard, though there were others still there, I suppose. I was warmed under a spotlight, and glowing slightly myself just then, if only from Bernard's reflection.

I went to Bernard's a week after the party to discuss working for him. I'd already driven by his house a few times by then, to make sure I'd be on time; the fancy part of town was new to me, and a little scary. In truth, I was already picturing my way out of a ground-floor apartment in Warwick with curtains the color of wheat, damp carpets, and a window that revealed only ankles and dogs' paws, and into the green and white house on Power Street that grew on the top of a hill. It had a porch as wide as a boat's deck and narrow shutters taller than me, windows so wide you could step right through them. A big house is the space you take up in the world, the piece you own; on a late afternoon, I'd seen Bernard reading the paper in front of the window that looked over the city.

I don't know if Bernard was nervous like I was that day—it seems not only unlikely, but laughable if you know him—but he cleared his throat a lot as we talked, and sometimes stopped in the middle of a sentence to pluck a feather of lint off his black wool pants. When I talked, he felt the terrain of spots on his head, and appeared surprised that there was no hair running through his fingers. He had more books than I'd ever seen, I said, most without jackets, library-like, and when he told me that he'd read every one of them, I didn't think it was really possible, but I didn't think he was lying either. He meant it in spirit, I suppose, which is the real truth, in the same way I say I'd give my life for Bernard now. Bernard slipped his fingertips into the pockets of his jacket and looked out the window onto Power Street. He was expecting his son Cam, he explained.

"Here's what I'm after," Bernard finally said. He didn't look at me when he talked, but I knew that he was taking in every inch. He straightened a painting of his dead wife Edith over the fireplace. Her hair was flattened in low waves around her face, and she looked like the kind of woman who was perfect all the time. I pulled my skirt down over a blossoming run in my stockings, and ran my tongue over my teeth to make sure there were no chips of lipstick there.

"Not a nurse, no, not precisely a secretary. What would I call it—" He stroked his mustache, though I knew he wasn't at a loss for words, but just pretending for some reason, "—a companion, an assistant. I live alone. I'm very busy, I have a lot of obligations and meetings to attend, and not enough time to take care of everything." This, I saw, was as close as he'd ever get to admitting he was old. He stood tall for a man his age, and his chest seemed to rise a little. "You understand? Live-in. Room, board, and a salary."

I'd done lots of things in my life, enough to know that what you do doesn't say anything about what you're worth. I'd been a manager at a ticket outlet, a job that left my hands stained purple for months, once an assistant to a man in a crayon factory because I thought it would be interesting—it wasn't. When I met Bernard, I was a secretary at a temp agency for middle-manager types, skilled labor, and how the place depressed me. A beautiful view of the Seekonk River from an office twelve stories up, and all day long, a parade of people with horrible stories, bad clothes, and terrible needs. Everything about it was wrong; they were trying to stay dignified, and hold on, but it made me dread seeing them. Every day, it made me think of my divorce and the curdled taste it left on my tongue in the morning, of not having a baby of my own. It also made me think of my mother, as though I'd gone all the way back to my beginning. She could be nasty on a beautiful day without even noticing.

Cam let himself into his father's house. I heard some rustling in the front hall, the swish of nylon running pants, the flipping of a thick stack of mail I'd seen on the table next to Bernard's hat. When he came into the living room, Cam stopped as though he hadn't expected to see me. Several letters stuck awkwardly out of the pocket of his pants.

"What do you have there?" Bernard asked his son.

Cam patted his pockets. "Letters that were supposed to come to me," he said, and then turned to where I was sitting. Bernard scowled a little, and cleared his throat again. "So, has my father told you what we're looking for?"

"Pretty much." My stomach had begun to hurt from sucking it in so long. "A companion, someone to take care of things."

Cam raised his eyebrows at me, and then began to talk very fast. Several times Bernard started to speak, but Cam kept on going, and each time his voice rose a little at his father's attempts. "This is a big place. Too big, too much money to keep up, but he won't sell."

"I don't blame him," I said. "If this was my place—I mean, you should have seen where I grew—"

Cam bit the corner of his lip. "Anyway, I live forty minutes away, which is too far to keep on top of things. He needs someone . . ."

"Closer," I said.

"In the house." Cam talked about his father, right in front of him, like he'd talk about a dog, or a baby. It made me think of how my father called my mother The She, and not like you say The Sun, The Stars, My Love.

It's the little things that break you, and Cam, in his tennis outfit with his ungraspable edges, wanted me to know about his father; he needed help using the can opener, going to the post office, doing the laundry, driving, zipping up, remembering the Metamucil. Each detail sent a pulse across Bernard's pale lips. His son, I realized, was the one person who made Bernard weak, and I didn't think that was right. He picked away at his father's pride.

"Well," I said, and stood right next to Cam, because one thing I learned from my ex is that you have to stand up to men, "there are some things all of us need help with. Big and little. It doesn't mean anything about a person. Seems to me your father's like all of us, he just wants a little company."

Before I left that afternoon, Bernard showed me the room where I'd be sleeping. It had a small window with a half circle on top, and through it I could see the backyard. I almost expected to see Cam there, waiting for something. But he had left by then for his tennis game, and later to his condo by the water in Jamestown, where he had lived alone since his divorce.

"His second divorce," Bernard said.

I know Bernard saw *something* when he looked at me in the purple light of the room and talked about his son, saw more than a slightly overweight woman, wearing glasses with a scratched left lens, and her best dress. I was sure he saw *me,* and if I was needed by him to heat his soup or type his letters, take him to the supermarket and the movies, to sit with him during the hardest hours of the day because his son didn't want to, or couldn't, or wasn't allowed to—well, that was something enormous to me. (I suppose I was hearing my mother, asking, "I raised you to change the pissy bedsheets of an old man?" but I turned away from her.)

From the start, every Monday, I drove Bernard in his Buick to Jacobs Plastics in Warren. He insisted that I park right in front of the entrance so that my tires were on the green welcome mat. Cam sent his secretary out to collect his father and sit me by the receptionist's desk with a cup of Cremora coffee and a copy of an in-flight magazine. Sometimes he sent her back out to hand me my paycheck, which he'd signed in a faint blue signature. Other times Cam handed the check to me himself when he walked us to the car, his hand hovering, but never touching his father's back. They discussed some last-minute business, and then Cam stood watching until I pulled the car onto Division Avenue. He reminded me of someone who'd won a staring contest, bleary-eyed for nothing, and a little smug with victory.

"What's he waiting for? Why does he just stand there?" I asked Bernard, who was foul with me after those times with his son. He didn't answer and sucked on a peppermint Lifesaver he always carried. When he bit down, I often wondered what had cracked, the candy or his tooth.

I thought how once I'd told Cam that I heard his father moaning, making the noise of a wounded animal. I told him I had run upstairs, seen Bernard sitting on the toilet with the door open, and how much it had scared me to see his chest resting on his knees. (And oh, those pants at his ankles, drooping over his shoes and spilling onto the tile floor. My hands at my temples, feeling my own pulse.) "But then I realized how this bending over helped." I showed Cam with my hand, a slowly closing mouth. "Makes things easier. That will be us not too long from now."

I thought Cam was close to tears. "Jesus Christ," he said, suddenly, "you might consider giving my father the privacy and respect he deserves. That's what I pay you for."

I had humiliated Cam in a way I didn't understand, and for weeks he turned away when we talked.

"He has such an expectant look on his face all the time," I said to Bernard as we drove away from Jacobs Plastics. "It's like he wants us to take him with us, but he doesn't want to come. Does he like anybody? Does he hate *everyone* or is it just me?" I didn't know how much I could say about Cam to Bernard. "He has so much unfinished business."

Bernard sighed, but his face was angry and tight when he turned to me. "You're wrong. He's an extremely capable businessman," he said. "Runs the place just like I did. Otherwise, I wouldn't have given him the company, now would I have, Lila."

I knew Cam poked through the house when we weren't there. I could feel his touch on my things, my pillow, his thumbprint on the half-sandwich I'd left in the fridge. It made me crazy that he'd take his father out without telling me. I'd come back from the store or out of my room and call Bernard's name, frantic, thinking of sick animals retreating into crawl spaces to die, finally furious and shaking. Of course, Bernard went with him, and no one was required to tell me, Cam pointed out. Always there was the threat, the reminder of my mereness.

I began to take Bernard on long car rides without destination because it was easiest, when I had the feeling that Cam was going to show up to correct me, or stand unyielding in front of his father. When we would finally return home, in the early and warm summer evening, we would carry the scent of Woodman's fried clams with us, and a necklace or a shell box Bernard had insisted on buying me. After Bernard was in bed, I'd swear I could smell Cam in the hallway of the dark house. People talk about the ghosts of dead babies not by how they look, white-sheeted like little Caspers, but how they smell, like a puff of powder in a blanket, and the tang of sweet urine in the air.

One evening after a trip to Point Judith and the crooked mouth of the harbor, I asked Bernard what the worst thing he'd ever done was. "One bad thing," I said. Bernard had corns, so I was chafing away with a pumice stone at the yellow skin, tough as the top of a dried fig. As I knelt in front of him, his foot rested on my bent leg. "Just name one."

Some people will tell you, glad to finally be rid of it. Others, well, Bernard was like them, and he clucked his tongue to make fun of me. He could be cruel when he felt like it—smart people can do that—teasing me for all I didn't know and what I believed in—prayers, diets, the power of positive thinking, questions like this.

"Nothing," he answered quickly.

My mother too, when she got old, bit her words off like Bernard, as if they tasted bad. "Yup" was the only thing she said to me right before she died. I'd spent months begging her to talk, to move her jaw against the pillow of flesh that was her double chin, but she'd never liked me and wasn't going to start then.

"Everyone does something awful, sometime," I said. A girl, an only child, not loved by her mother? "No one leads a perfect life."

"Okay." Bernard pressed on his eyelids. "Edith slapped Cam across the face. Twice actually, right and left. Smack, smack, smack." I felt the wind of his moving hand.

"That's three times." I said. "Smack, smack, smack."

"That was probably the worst thing *she* ever did."

"I didn't ask about her, though. I asked about you. Now relax your toes. You're all clenched up." I massaged the balls of his yeasty smelling feet.

"That feels very nice, Lila." He paused. "That was the first time Cam had ever been hit; he must have been about five. We were in a different house then, a little place on Sixth Street near the hospital. I don't know why Edith did it—Cam was a good boy, a little lonely, not very good in school, but a good boy. I was downstairs at the time. Edith was generally a very controlled person. I made that rule in the house, to be in control."

He let me dig out the pasty stuff under his toenails. "I don't see how you can make a rule about that," I said.

Bernard put his head way back and stared at the ceiling. His throat bobbed, quivered a little as he spoke softly. "I've never felt right about the whole thing. A terrible thing to do to a child."

"Well, I got slapped plenty as a kid, but you move on." I was waiting for him to ask me about myself—he said he liked to know how people like me grew up—but I could tell there wasn't a lot of room left in his life to hear all my sorrows. I ran my hand up and down his calf, under the twill of his pants. He made a strange cooing noise. "Bernard? You still with us?"

He jiggled his foot and his voice was squeezed. "She hit him a lot, and then she'd keep him home because his eye was black." Bernard finally looked down at me, but his face was mostly in shadows, shiny with tears, and he touched my cheek. "You know, what could I do? What's done is done now. I haven't thought about this in years. Cam's grown up."

"But Cam's not done," I said, excitedly, and cradled his foot against my breast. I had to hold onto this understanding of why Cam acted the way he did. We weren't so different; I know the damage that's been done. "He's not finished," I said. "That's why he always has that look on his face, waiting for something from you. For you to save him."

Bernard didn't say anything. "Do you want me to do the other foot?" I asked. He could be a cold bastard at times and my knees ached. I poked hard with my file, but he didn't wince. "You could tell him you're sorry, Bernard. That's all, tell him he's okay, that you're sorry, that you love him."

Bernard let out a pinched laugh and drew in his breath suddenly. "Cuckle me, Lila." His fingers tapped on his thighs, then my cheek. He had a voice of tears, his heart had broken.

"What?"

"Cuckle me."

I rose from my knees and moved slowly toward him. Patches of Bernard's skin were as cold and smooth as an empty perfume bottle I once found in the snow and brought home. Old flesh looks almost dead, but practically newborn too, an amazing thing in the tones of a lilac night. All men are different and the same in most ways, and the man was alive, he smelled of blood under skin, tasted like bread and water, his fingers touched my hair.

We understood something then, that old men die soon, and

each day had to become as full, as thick and colorful as paintings lit by candlelight. You can forget about friends, and things you have to do, and all you've missed and done wrong, and think you can't make up. Love surprised us, we saved each other and ourselves.

We've just crossed the Connecticut border, not even an hour from Providence, and something's happened to the heat in the Escort. My feet are cold, my McDonald's coffee is the same temperature as the air and as tasteless as snow. There's no whoosh of hot air coming from the vent, just a jumbling of something that sounds like pebbles. Bernard's been saying for months he'd like to get me a new car, and I should have taken him up on it. He gives me a little money now and then, presses my hand, says, "Take it." He doesn't have to tell me not to say anything to Cam. Bernard is talking in his end-of-sleep, waking from his nap. Tiny diamonds coat his eyelashes. I like to think that he's dreaming of love, babbling away in it, like a baby in the bath.

"Honey," I say, and touch Bernard on the shoulder, "it's a little cold. You warm enough in here? Something's happened to the heat."

Bernard looks out the window, sees the signs for Foxwoods Casino, one after the other as we barrel down Interstate 95. You'd have to be a hundred-and-one to miss them, and we've never driven this way before.

"Connecticut," he pronounces, and sits up taller in the seat. "The Indians. They let children use the slot machines."

"That doesn't sound right," I say.

Bernard is shivering, though he doesn't admit it, and stares ahead at the turquoise rise of the casino half a mile away through the trees. The place throws a shadow on us, Bernard is a little amazed by it, and a bubble forms at the corner of his mouth. It makes me think of all the things he's seen happen in his lifetime. Airplanes were remarkable, the atomic bomb unthinkable, and television shattering all quiet, but I think it must be the small, fairytale things that really stun him: ATM machines that spit money, watches that talk, huge turquoise buildings in the middle of nowhere, rising like castles.

"We should gamble today, Lila. See what everyone's talking about. Millions of dollars a day, I've read," he says.

"Please, Bernard, you don't gamble." I know nothing about cars, but I have a bad feeling about mine at the moment, that water's going to start gushing from the rusted bottom, split open like a rotten melon if we don't stop. "You don't even play the lottery." But he checks my tickets during the evening news, and never tells me I've lost, as though he can't stand to disappoint me.

Bernard insists we stop, and I pull up to the mouth of the vast parking lot only because I'm not quite sure what to do about the car, which lurches and heaves under my foot. The black ground shines through the just-plowed snow, and the place is so bright it looks like a lure to draw in the weak and hopeful. Bernard waves me to a space not too far from what looks like a bus shelter. Several people are already standing there, and when their eyes aren't turned to the casino or straining to see the shuttle bus coming up the hill, they're checking their plastic cups full of quarters, their complimentary drink tickets, wiping their noses. With stiff knees and heavy coats, they climb onto the shuttle bus, and we follow. Two women coyly shift to the left to make room for Bernard, and he smiles at them. When the bus pulls up to the entrance, everyone rushes out; they're suddenly lively and they know where they're going.

"A monstrosity," Bernard announces, as we ride the escalator past the two-story high glass Indian who is planted in a garden of plastic pines, his arrow pointed up as though it's going to burst right through the skylight and end up smashing someone's windshield on 95. There's the whir and ping of the slots behind us, the haze of cigarette smoke, the windows that face onto untouched hills. The whole place makes me dizzy, as if I just got off an airplane and don't really believe I'm where they say I am. Bernard is talking statistics, politics, judgments, addictions, one thing right after another, but won't turn to the cave of noise behind us. I'm not sure I've ever seen him out of place like this. He seems not to know which way to turn.

There were times I forgot that Bernard was eighty-five, an old man. There were unpredictable days of fatigue and irritation and bad body smells, days when he'd talk about Cam, pride and pity all mixed until he'd fall into a moroseness I could barely lift him out of. Cam would circle his father, and the way he tilted his head to get Bernard to look at him, to say something, was painful to see.

One morning about a month ago, I took a load of clean laundry into the living room where I was going to sort it and watch television. Bernard was on the phone upstairs, making his usual round of important calls, and I heard the wheels of his chair hum across the wooden floor of his office as he rocked himself back and forth. On the green velvet couch, I folded his underwear, my sweatpants, his dark socks, my nightgown, my bra.

"Lila," he called, almost a whisper.

I went out into the hall and looked to the landing where he always stood to ask me if the mail had arrived yet, or if I'd bring him some soup. That morning the sun from the window behind him lit up the skin on his head and made the outline of his body's gentle collapse glow in pale yellow. My hands went to my lips.

"What's wrong, Bernard?" I started climbing the stairs, slowly. Sometimes he was like a bird, and if I moved too fast, he startled.

"I'm a little tired. I thought I might lie down for a few minutes."

"That sounds fine," I said, thinking that he'd just talked to Cam. (I knew how much he'd been wanting to say the right thing to his son.) "I'll help you."

A few minutes later, on his bed, his breathing was like falling sheets upon my back, over my eyes, on the back of my thighs.

"Cuckle me," he whispered. His soft fingers and his stiff hands formed arches on my skin, dots of warmth through my sweater, the one he'd picked out for me because he said it matched my eyes.

Cam had been watching. I saw his reflection in the glass door on one of the bookshelves in the hall outside Bernard's room. He was like water poured on that glass, wavy, here and then gone so quickly. It left me parched, feeling burned and cold at the same time, which was wrong, I thought. Because this is right. No one can say it isn't, and I looked at Bernard, who was asleep, his fists curled under his chin.

Cam was sitting in the living room, on the green couch, squeezed between the piles of folded laundry when I came down-stairs. He sat the same way his father always did, legs crossed, dangling toes, pointing down.

"I didn't hear you come in, Cam. You shouldn't sneak like that. You're going to give your father a heart attack." I turned off the television and gathered up the laundry in my arms.

"I let myself in." His voice had a little wave to it. "Did you know that it's a beautiful day out there? You have all the curtains shut, so I guess you wouldn't have noticed. I thought I might take my father out for lunch. He'd enjoy the walk, the fresh air would be good for him. What do you think?"

"Actually, he's asleep. He was feeling a little tired this morning. We had a busy day yesterday." Cam raised his eyebrows. "So I don't think this is the best time. But I'll tell him you were here."

Cam looked at his watch. "It's only eleven. Do you think it's all right for him to be asleep at this hour? I'm interested in your opin-ion, if you think it's normal."

"Normal? I don't know what you expect at his age," I said. My throat tightened. "He can sleep whenever he wants, with-out people fussing or worrying about what it means. That's what I think."

Cam stood up. He was wearing a dark suit with a red silk hand-kerchief in his breast pocket. He looked and smelled as though he was going to meet a woman, and I wondered what he thought of himself when he got up in the morning, if he imagined someone waiting for him at night, if that's what he wanted. "You expect too much of him, Lila. I'm telling you this as nicely as I can. I'm just not sure what you think is going to happen."

I was angry all of a sudden, scared too, stumbling to hit back. "What's happened is that I've decided not to bring him to your office on Mondays anymore. He's exhausted by the time we get home, upset. He tries with you the best he can, but sometimes I wonder what you want from him, and what you do to him in there when you don't get it."

Cam laughed and shrugged. "What *I* do, Lila? You're asking what *I* do? What do *you* do?"

"I love him," I said. Cam shook his head. "He loves me, I make him happy. I get him out, I show him things. Look, my mother slapped me plenty as a child too, and I had a dark part, just like you, but look at me."

"That old story," he said and turned to me. I was still clutching his father's boxer shorts, all our things washed together, to my chest. "You want me to look at you? A forty-something woman spending time with a man who's almost ninety? You're not filled with love—and God knows he isn't—you're filled with shit, Lila. Something pathetic."

Cam walked over to the big window that faced Power Street and opened the curtains. He was right, it was a beautiful day, cold but bright. I thought I saw in his eyes that he wished his father dead for giving away what should have been his. "I almost—*almost*—feel a little sorry for you," he said, "but I have to think of him first. You're going to have to leave—this house, and my father."

Bernard finally turns away from the casino window. "I'd like to use the bathroom," he says. The first one we find is for the handicapped, and he goes in. There are a lot of layers to be undone on Bernard, and I'd like to help, but I know that I have to wait right outside the door, patient, until he calls me. People smile at me—I'm holding Bernard's coat—when they see me waiting dutifully for my handicapped someone to return.

"Lila," Bernard says. The door is shut, his voice is faint.

"Bernard?"

"Lila, I need you."

When I go into the bathroom, Bernard's standing near the toilet—there's only one in the room—and he's struggling with the zipper of his pants. There's a single square of toilet paper in the bowl and I can't stop staring as it begins to fold in on itself and then disappear in the water. In a few seconds, there's no trace of it at all.

Maybe I'm tired—we had a long night last night—or worried about the car and what we'll do, or foggy from all that smoke, but I'm chilled and sweating like a sick kid, and suddenly full of heavy sorrow. I realize how little I ever think of Bernard's dying. Dead, well that's inevitable—I have thought about life without him, I've had to. But dying.

"My zipper, Lila," Bernard says again. I can hear the slot machines sucking in and spitting out coins even through these walls.

I flush the toilet, but something has colored the room, as if I'm wearing a pair of purple-tinted sunglasses. I straighten Bernard's pants, zip his zipper, turn him around by the shoulders and lead him out of the bathroom.

There's a bench by the window, a low turquoise thing with a fringe that tickles my legs when I sit down. I've stopped listening to Bernard, who is telling me to get up. The plastic is slick and cold, and I hate the dirty feel of it. When I lie back, my sweater lifts so a bit of skin shows above the waist of my pants.

"Lila, where's my coat?" Bernard asks. I feel too much of everything to answer. He leans over and pulls down my sweater, leans over to protect *me*. His eyes are fixed on my face, and I wonder what he's thinking, and where we'll go now.

Hours before her best friend died, my wife sold the fourteen-room brick Colonial on Cole Avenue that she'd been showing to clients for over a year. When Eleanor called to tell me about it, her voice was breathless, but loud enough, I noticed, with each word carefully and triumphantly articulated, so that her colleagues could hear even as they pretended they weren't listening. I looked up from the work in front of me and saw a reflection in the window opposite my desk. It was a reflection of myself, naturally, with Providence like lush foliage behind me, but at that moment it could have been Ellie's face I saw instead of my own. We were at times almost like one person, with her eyes that become greener when she's feeling accomplished and excited, her perfectly rounded chin, her crown of red curls.

It was much later that day—in fact, I was getting ready to leave and my briefcase was sitting open-mouthed on the chair—when Ellie called again, this time to tell me that Pamela had died. Pam had been at home, propped up in a chair in front of the television, while her husband fixed her lunch in the other room—"As if she could have eaten it anyway," Ellie added, bitterly. I imagined my wife's mouth tightening, mimicking Pam's.

Several weeks earlier on a Sunday evening, Pam and her husband Peter had been at our house for dinner. Despite all the years of knowing each other, as a foursome we were still somewhat and, at this point, acceptably awkward together. Pam and Ellie didn't know how or want to integrate us into their intimacy—which at times made them as oblivious as little girls. Peter and I were observers as usual that evening, stuck on the couch, stuck fixing drinks, and our talk was about them, and around them. I knew how sick Pam was; I could see it in the platinum glare of her eyes and the way she sank into her dress bright as a circus, but we acted as though there was nothing wrong. The four of us joked and gossiped. When we sat down at the table, Pam's eyes fixed on the basket of yellow and green gourds Ellie had taken the time to arrange, then on the cobalt blue glasses that caught the light, then on her pale hand on the paler tablecloth. She never picked up her spoon to taste the chicken soup, never rippled its surface. Later, I dumped the full bowl down the sink.

I had watched Ellie at the stove that morning as she began the soup for her friend. She wore her faded blue bathrobe and had that determined and slightly furrowed look on her face as she sliced carrots and celery and the blade of the knife butted against her thumb. If I knew that Pam wouldn't be around much longer, and if Ellie knew it too—and of course she had to, they must have discussed it—we didn't say anything about it, she didn't speak of it to me then. Ellie hummed along to the radio, so she wouldn't have to open her mouth and speak, I thought. I couldn't watch this and went outside to work on the bushes, which had grown so high that summer and fall that their shadows fell on the house. Outside, that single detail of chicken soup—just that, and my sweet wife's sweet notion of the simplest cure for her friend's cruelest cancer—gripped my heart. I looked back into the kitchen through the sliding glass door. Ellie had left the room by then, but steam rose in steady curative clouds from the pot.

I tried to soothe my wife when she called to tell me about Pam, but the women had been best friends for almost thirty years. They talked practically every day on the telephone, often more than that. Sometimes I heard Ellie tell Pam something about herself that surprised me—not confidences I shouldn't have heard, but half-formed insecurities, unapologetic comments about friends they had in common, speculations of no consequence, feelings about our daughter—the kind of things men don't tell each other. They talked about their work as well (which is what I talk about with my friends)—Ellie in real estate, Pam at her painting—their successes and grievances and choices, and at times I heard Ellie wonder out loud how she'd ended up in real estate. Magically, it seemed to me, enviably even, their words to each other smoothed the edges off discontent and anxiety. At times I was vaguely jealous of their friendship—but if I heard these things from Ellie, would I know what to say? For the most part, the rhythm of their evening conversation was a soothing routine for me, and our life.

I heard the right words leave my mouth, but my mind was stuck on a single, incongruous thought at the moment, which was that despite all my wife's success—two golden decades in the real estate business when everyone else scrambled—she still had no office of her own, something she'd often complained about to Pam. What was sad to me just then was not simply Pamela's death but that Ellie had to cry in public, in the swirl of things. Her profound moment was painfully self-conscious; she lowered her voice to talk, she tried to swallow her sobs. I knew that as soon as we hung up she'd turn to accept pats of condolence from the people she worked with. They were her friends and had been for years, and she would touch them back with equally strained gestures, because my wife was nothing if not gracious and thoughtful, thinking of her place, other people, and the next day.

"I know it's a cliché, Jack," she said, "but I didn't even get to say good-bye to Pam. I assumed I was going to talk to her tonight."

"You couldn't have said good-bye anyway."

Ellie laughed at herself. I could tell that she was straightening up then, aligning her spine, her head, her feet, and smoothing the tailored cherry-red jacket I'd watched her put on that morning.

"Are you okay?" I asked. "Should I pick you up?"

"My face is a mess," she answered, and cleared her throat, "but I'm all right. I'll be fine." She paused then and let out another half-laugh. I could hear the noise of her office behind her. "God, now who am I going to *talk* to?"

She hadn't asked the kind of question that really wants an answer—although I could have said *me,* you can always talk to *me*—and so we said good-bye. I drove home, and as I pulled up in front of the house I saw that Ellie was already there. The same lights she always turned on were on, and I knew that she had probably changed out of her work clothes because that was the first thing she always did. This was the good, comfortable life we'd made I saw in front of me, my house on a slight hill with a wide, hard-earned view, the place where we'd raised our daughter Moira, where we intended to stay through older, easy years. I thought of my wife's victory that morning—it had been an arduous sale—and her great loss that afternoon, and how even the smoothest of lives, the best marriages, are filled with dips and rises to be ridden together.

Of course Ellie was sad; I expected that. For the first few weeks, during the part of the evening she would have normally spent talking to her friend, Ellie seemed—literally—aimless and mute. One minute she'd stand at the kitchen door with her face pressed to the glass in a way that made me want to cry, not hearing a word I said, and just as I was about to put my hand on her shoulder and turn her around, she would start to rearrange the knives in the knife rack, or pull the yellowing leaves off the ficus tree and gather them in her hands.

At other times I found myself looking at Ellie with an ugly blend of frustration and anger, willing her to do something, to respond to me.

"Didn't you and Pam ever talk about what it would be like?" I asked one evening as I stood over her. The morning's newspaper was open in front of her on the table, but she hadn't turned a page for a long time. "How could you not have talked about what it would be like for *you*? In all the time, you never pictured it?" I heard my sharp voice fill the kitchen, and when Ellie didn't look up or answer, I bent over and put my face next to hers. "Ellie, please, I want to help you," I said, "but I don't know how. I don't know what to do, what to say."

She reached up and touched my face, but still could not bring herself to speak. I knew then that the shape and depth of her loss was unimaginable to me, and I didn't know what I could replace it with.

One Sunday evening almost three months after Pam's death, we sat at our table again with Peter. These dinners—and Ellie's insistence on including him in our Thanksgiving, inviting him to go to the movies with us, or her calling him just to say hello or offer him part of a bushel of apples we'd picked—were our way of taking care of him, our duty. His acceptances were dutiful also, and he'd show up with his long, narrow face, his eyes toward the floor. We were a morose threesome, and I couldn't wait for him to leave.

When I came back from picking up Chinese food for dinner, Ellie put the cartons on the table. She slapped them down hard and carelessly, so that the seams bulged and began to leak.

"Sweetheart," I said, and held onto her wrist, "careful." Peter nodded. "There's no rush."

Ellie pulled her hand away from me and ripped open a container because she couldn't bend the metal handle easily enough—this from a woman who would arrange crackers on a plate even when there were just two of us and we could have eaten out of the box.

"Ellie, do you have any beer?" Peter asked, once we were seated and eating. His eyes lifted from his plate long enough to look at her.

She shot him a stare of resentment and sucked on a chopstick.

Her chair was pushed back so that her knees rested against the table. She wasn't going to move.

"Let me check," I said, and got up. I put my hand on his shoulder first, and then touched Ellie's as I went to look in the refrigerator.

At one point while we were eating—and Peter was droning on about his students so that I was making designs on my plate with a chopstick to amuse myself and Ellie was looking out the window—the phone rang. Ellie picked it up too eagerly—this was a sudden energy, her old energy, when she hadn't wanted to answer it for weeks. I was sure she would tell Sally—a friend from the office—that she would call back later because we had a guest, but she took the phone out of the room. I watched the cord tighten and uncoil, and I knew, from having seen this practically every night for so many years when she talked to Pam, that she had found a place to sit and she intended to talk for a long, long time.

From the other room, Ellie laughed in an intimate but I knew forced way, and then roared with fake indignation at something she'd heard. I smiled weakly at Peter and shrugged as though to make some dumb comment about women and their telephones that we both understood, but he just continued to pick at his food. I thought desperately of what to say to him and how to cover up Ellie's chatter, and to let him know how sorry I was about everything, and that I knew this was rude of my wife. But after a few minutes I gave up when I understood that finally Peter would not be able to bear us after tonight, or my wife and her friends, or our life that really was going to survive this loss—though we too suffered—while his had hit some kind of terrible wall. Peter left before dessert, while there was food still cooling on his plate. This is the kindest cut, really, I thought to myself when at the front door we nodded to each other and said goodbye, see you later. This is what my wife has to do, I wanted to add, and you have to understand her pain too, understand that she is rearranging things now, fixing, replacing. I felt a relief—for each of us—when he drove away.

Later, upstairs in our bedroom, Ellie announced that she

couldn't stand to be with Peter anymore. "And the way he talks on and on about his job," she said, pulling a flannel nightgown over her head and then shaking out her hair, "it's enough to make me scream. I never knew he was so unbearably boring. Well, I suppose I did, but I never paid much attention with Pam around. Now, my God."

She practically tore the covers back off our bed and got in. She picked up her appointment book which she had brought upstairs with her, as she did every night before going to sleep or making love or watching television. "Are you coming to bed?" She flipped through the pages and tapped the pen against her teeth.

"In a minute." I went into the bathroom and thought of Peter in his empty house by then, and how hunched and hunkered in his brown coat he'd looked as he walked to his car. When I brushed my teeth, I saw myself in the mirror and was surprised to see how tense I looked, and how even with my mouth open, my jaw was tight.

I heard Ellie talking. "Jesus, how do you think Pam stood him all those years?"

I left the bathroom and stood over the bed. "The man's wife just died. He's supposed to make brilliant conversation all the time?"

"He could at least make an effort."

"And what about you taking that call during dinner? Is that your idea of an effort? Anyway, you always liked Peter—you're not being honest about this."

"You're wrong. I never liked him, but he was Pam's husband, so what could I do about it?" She scribbled something in her book—an appointment, a sales pitch, a trick to remember a client's favorite brand of appliance—slapped it shut, and then looked up at me.

"It was cruel, Ellie," I said.

"I know it was," she sighed, "and I'm sorry." I saw that she was close to tears. "But look, Pam's dead, and he's not. He's the one who's here, and I can't stand that."

Ellie opened her arms to me for the first time in months. I

slipped in next to my wife, and for a few minutes pressed my face to Ellie's almond-soaped skin.

"I wonder if people would say the same thing about me if you died," I said after a few minutes, "that they tolerated me because of you. I think the hardest part of death is being left alone."

"I won't die and leave you like that." She spoke in a voice that reminded me of how she used to talk to Moira when she was touched and teary. Ellie sat up, took off her nightgown, and threw it on the floor. She turned off the light and began to stroke my head—I thought of the white cat we'd had once who used to seek out Ellie's lap—and her fingers danced lightly on my scalp where my hair had thinned to almost nothing and I was aroused. Suddenly she pulled my face to her chest. I loved my wife too much to look up and see the sorrow on her face so I held her as tightly as she held me, in gratitude for what we had, and in relief that her pain would finally begin to ebb after tonight.

I had known from the day I met her in an undergraduate history class—I'd watched her foot slip in and out of her flat shoe for an hour—that Eleanor had a fierce but slightly unfortunate intelligence that allowed her to do anything she wanted, but cursed her with a dissatisfaction with anything she did. History was a whim, it didn't hold her long, while I, held or not, did what was expected. Amazingly, I was not a whim to this independent curious woman half my size; we got married. For the years when Moira was young and at home all day, Eleanor was a thoughtful mother, but sometimes I saw behind her smile as she helped Moira with blocks on the kitchen floor or chalk on the easel, or I heard hidden in her voice as she sang our baby to sleep that she was thinking vaguely of other things, things I thought she wanted but maybe did not know yet herself.

Selling houses was something real for her. She had no great interest in architecture, sales, or money, and a certain snobbish disdain for the profession that I happened to share with her. But it was the first job that really held her—simply, I think, because of the changing challenges—and I thought I saw some of this earlier worrisome dreaminess disappear. Even after twenty years of watching her operate, I was still amazed by her inventiveness in matching people to places. She would be out of the house by seven in the morning to show a couple from New York the best coffee bar in Providence (which incidentally, would turn out to be around the corner from the house she eventually sold them).

For years, I've successfully worked at the thing I was trained to do in law school—be the litigious faction in tragic family feuds, take away an old man's power over his own life, tick off liens on dusty estates. The steadiness is what I'm good at, what's made me admired and satisfied, why I'm a senior partner. I admit this about myself when I used to hate it. Between the two of us, Ellie and I often said to each other, privately, after a party or on a walk, we had Providence covered; she knew who lived behind the doors, and I knew what they did there.

We spent New Year's Eve at Sally's party, our first time out after weeks of long days at work and longer, quieter nights at home. Ellie, lovely in a black dress and silver bracelets, sat stiff and solitary on a couch, and drank too much because she was too sad to talk to anyone. From where I stood across the room, talking with friends, I watched her eyes wander over the furniture, the self-conscious, collected decor, her colleagues and friends making conversation and checking their watches. Sally, loud and full of hostess-confidence, waved Ellie to join her several times, and I saw in Ellie's polite refusal, in the small shake of her head, a disconcerting detachment. These were her friends, but she had no desire to be in the circle with them, and I had no desire to leave it.

Still, I went to sit on the couch next to her. "Would you like to go home now?" I asked Ellie. I took away her glass of wine—she didn't protest or even seem to notice. Of course I understood all this, I told myself, her best friend was dead. Last year at this time, I remembered seeing Ellie and Pam holding on to each other, laughing, and when midnight came Ellie naturally turned to me and we kissed. Now, on this night four months after Pam's death, my wife's mourning for her friend had submerged her—again. People told me this was perfectly normal, that the timing of grief was unpredictable—and I had certainly seen that through better and worse weeks with Ellie—but moments like this were almost defeating for me. "Or we could stay—it's just about midnight," I added.

"Let's go home," she said, and we got our coats. I had to thank Sally for both of us, as Ellie was already in the front hall, her hand on the doorknob, with no intention of looking at what she'd left behind.

Toward the end of January, I came home from work earlier than usual and was surprised to find Ellie playing solitaire in the kitchen. This was something she often did—I had always seen it as a sign of her competitiveness, even with herself, while playing alone held no appeal to me—but that afternoon, when only the small greasy light over the stove was turned on, it seemed strange, too internal. She was keeping score on the back of an envelope, and the columns twisted over and around the paper.

I wondered why, out of all the things my wife could have chosen to do, she would be playing cards in the half-dark. From the number of used tea bags bleeding on the counter, from Ellie's shapeless sweatpants, sweatshirt, and defuzzed pink slippers, I knew that she had been home for hours—and that this game of cards was all she felt up to.

"I thought you had a late house appointment," I said casually, and leaned over to kiss her. She didn't look up from her cards. "Isn't that what you said this morning? The house on Upton?"

"I canceled. Well, actually, I let Sally take it for me." Her voice was thick, as though she hadn't talked in hours, and she put down another card. I had never known her to either cancel an appointment—even in what I imagined was the worst time, right after Pam died—or give one away.

"You let Sally show the house?" I asked. I leafed through the mail Ellie hadn't bothered to open. "You've always said she's not aggressive, that sales slip away from her. Why would you let her take one of your houses? Isn't this an important one for you?"

"I'm just tired, okay?" Ellie bit her lip—she didn't need me to point out how strange this was of her, giving up an opportunity, especially one that might turn around a slow couple of months. "I didn't feel like showing it, talking to people, giving the same stupid speech over and over about wrapped asbestos pipes and forced hot air and oak sliders." She looked up at me, challenging. Her lips were very dry, as though she'd been breathing through her mouth.

"Ellie," I said, "I understand what you're going through, how hard this is for you. It's just not like you, that's all."

She paused. "*I'm* not like me."

I turned on the brightest light then, and began to make dinner. I found it hard to concentrate on what I was doing—peeling shrimp that kept slipping out of my hands—with the faint slapping of the cards punctuated by my wife's sighs. Slumped, with her chin almost touching her chest and her legs out in front of her, Ellie looked exactly like Moira as a sixteen-year-old.

"What does that mean, 'I'm not like me'?" I shouted and threw the shrimp into the sink. "What the hell does that mean?"

Ellie turned and looked at me. "I showed a house on the corner of Everett and Elmgrove this morning."

"And?" My voice was tight.

"To a couple from Texas—was it Texas? I don't remember— and we went into the kitchen. The woman looked in the cabinets—you know, they all do that, though who knows what they're looking for—and the man ran his fingers over the gaskets on the refrigerator and then the dishwasher, which seemed to embarrass his wife. She kept pulling at his arm and telling him to come on. It was pretty uncomfortable for all of us, one of those marriages you know is heading in the wrong direction."

"Maybe he's a plumber. Or he likes gaskets," I said, impatiently. I wanted to get things back on track; I didn't know where she was going with this. "Don't read too much into it."

"He doesn't want to move, that's obvious, and they were wasting my time, wasting each other's time. Anyway, they were having this hissing match I was trying to mediate, and the whole time I was thinking how little I cared about the house and the sale and them. At one point I looked at the counter over by the stove, and there were several enormous pieces of meat thawing on a platter. Who would eat all of that? There was a puddle of blood with a film of ice and oil on it, and all of a sudden I was sure I could smell the meat, that it was spoiled, and that I was going to be sick."

I looked at the sink full of shrimp mixed with their own shells. At that moment I could imagine Ellie in a strange kitchen staring at the meat and becoming even paler than she already was. I could almost taste the salt that must have risen to her mouth as her stomach turned, feel her need to curl up on the floor, or run away.

"I had to leave the room," she went on, her voice unsteady. "I let them look at the rest of the house by themselves. I've never done that before." It seemed that she had even scared herself. "Never once in all these years. I just didn't care about any of it."

I stood next to her and put the flat of my hand against her cheek, to hold her against me for a few seconds. "You feel warm," I said. "Maybe you should lie down."

"Don't." Ellie pulled away from me suddenly. "Don't diagnose me. For once, just listen to me, to what I'm saying."

"I am listening—and it sounds awful for you, it really does—but I've been listening for months," I said. "You're so angry, Ellie, you don't give me a chance."

"Of course I'm angry. You treat me like this is some kind of flu I've got, something I'll get over with a little help, but it isn't like that." She collected the cards in front of her and laid them out for another game.

"It's interesting—have I ever told you?" she went on. "People clean their houses before I come over but they forget to change the cat box, so that the first thing you smell when you walk in is shit, shit, and more shit. It doesn't matter that they've put flowers around or vacuumed the rug or sprayed air freshener in the toilet—the place stinks, it's horrible." She shook her head, and when she stopped, she looked at me. "And you know what I'm going to do next time? Tell them. I'll say, 'Your house smells of shit.'" Her face was red and angry. "'And I can't sell your house if it smells like shit.'" She pushed her chair back and left the room.

When I went to find her for dinner, she was in her flannel nightgown, the one that makes her look so tiny, asleep in bed, her fists curled under her chin. I ate dinner alone and stared at the envelope with Ellie's solitaire scores on it. After, in the kitchen with the lights out, I called Moira.

"Have you talked to your mother?" I started, and concentrated on keeping my voice steady. "How does she seem to you? You and she talk about things, about how she's doing?"

"Oh, Dad, her best friend just died," Moira said. "She's feeling pretty awful right now. She's been calling me a lot, actually. This morning at work she wanted to talk, to see if I'd gotten the earrings she'd sent, but I was busy, I really couldn't stay on. There were people in my office."

At the sound of Moira's voice, I felt like wailing—that's how disturbed I was by Ellie. "She didn't tell me she called you. You already talked to her then, okay? I'll let you go."

"Well, like I said, we really didn't talk for long, Dad." She paused. "It wasn't a good time; I told her that."

"I'm sure she understood." I cleared my throat as though to make way for what poured out so quickly. "I'm not sure what to do anymore. I'm afraid she's losing it, and I don't know how to help her. She needs to see someone. I'm worried, Moira, really worried." I heard voices behind my daughter, clearly a party that could no longer keep quiet in her tiny New York apartment. "You have guests," I said. "You should have said something right off. We'll talk another time."

"I'll call tomorrow," she promised. Could she hear just how much at a loss I was? "I'll call Mom before she leaves for work. Really, I will. Will you tell her how much I appreciate the earrings?"

I sat in the dark for a while, feeling the cold begin to creep around my ankles since I'd turned down the heat. When I went into the bedroom, Ellie was awake, sitting up in bed. I rubbed my face and busied with undressing so she couldn't see that I'd been crying. I mentioned that I'd done a little work I'd brought home, that I'd talked to Moira for only a second, and that she'd liked the earrings.

"They seemed perfect for her," Ellie said, "and I just felt like giving her something. What time is it anyway? I took one of your pills this afternoon—it made me so groggy."

I told her it was after ten. I tried not to think about her coming home to the empty house and fumbling around in the medicine cabinet. Why hadn't she come to me instead, called me out of a meeting if she had to, talked to me? I sat on the bed. Ellie smelled of restless sleep. "Do you want to see what a doctor has to say about all this?" I stroked her cool hand. "I know you miss Pam. I wish I could do something for you."

"There's really nothing to do." She looked down at her hand in mine. "I feel as though I've lost my balance—my footing would be more like it," she said, quietly, and moved toward me.

Ellie put her arms around me. If I was afraid that I was losing her then—which I was, and really, selfishly afraid of losing our life's balance together—I was also afraid that she was falling apart. The way she held onto me so desperately was terrifying and I could not hold her back.

One mid-morning my secretary called me out of a meeting. "Your wife," she whispered, her hand to her cheek, "is on the phone."

I rushed out to take the call. "Ellie," I asked, "is everything okay?"

"Oh, fine. I just wanted to say hi."

I coughed a tic of impatience. "Well, look, hi. Ell, I'm in the middle of something . . . can we talk later, at home?"

She made a kind of clicking sound with her mouth. "All you had to do was say you were busy," she said, and then added before she hung up, "It's nothing important."

Later that day I left the office to pick up a book I'd ordered for Moira's birthday. I wanted to get something special for my daughter—I knew that Ellie's constant calls were not easy for her. I was huffing through the cold when a flash of purple caught my eye as I passed the coffee shop I often went to on the mornings Ellie left the house early. The color made me stop and look through the foggy window more closely. The purple drew me into a sweet undefined memory for a second, like a smell, and I knew it was the same unusual hue of a fringed silk scarf I'd bought for Ellie years ago. I saw that it was Ellie's scarf, on Ellie of course, and that she was alone in this place we had never been to together, reading a magazine, her hair curling in the steam rising from her cup. I backed away from the window instead of going in to sit with Ellie, ashamed and scared because I didn't think I could stand to fail once again to give her what she needed, what she was trying to ask for.

I had always hurried home from my office. Now I was, out of choice and inefficiency, still at my desk late into the evening. I read weepy letters from clients, every plausible excuse for non-payment, official documents of horror. A five-year-old boy had fallen out of his stepfather's apartment window and died, and his grandparents were suing. I read the cases over and over as though I had become suddenly stupid; all other tragedy and grief seemed dull and distant in comparison to what was going on in my own life.

On these nights my colleagues, big men like me with thick middles and gentle, unhandsome faces, peered in at me with satisfaction—I had been smug and unsympathetic to their problems for so long. Their lives had all taken sour turns at some point; these offices were a refuge, and I understood that they knew better than to risk being away from them for long. At the end of the day, they bought me too many scotch-and-sodas at a club that was made to look like a law firm, with desks for tables and green-glass lamps. They appeared to take delight in the fact that I was finally one of them—they didn't want to go home either—but I wasn't like them at all. I loved my wife—I just couldn't bear to be with her. I wanted *more* of the Ellie I knew, *more* of my old life back, not less.

And then one day in early March, when the city was still pocked with black snow but the days were brighter, I was working on something at my desk and I had a powerful sense that Ellie was nearby. It was like waking up to find someone standing over you, and my heart beat too fast. I went to the window—I honestly thought I was going a little crazy—and saw the sun hovering over the Civic Center and the city divided by the highway. When I looked down fifteen stories, I saw traffic circling Kennedy Plaza, and among it, Ellie's little red car maneuvering in and out and then, eel-like, slipping into a parking space.

I watched her run across the street holding her purse down against her side, and take a wide step over a puddle in her high heels. I couldn't help thinking that something tragic had happened, and I wanted to hide, but all she wanted was to have lunch with me.

She leaned her hips against mine. "Just the two of us, Jack," she said. "It's been so long."

I started for an excuse, I fiddled in my pockets as though it was there. Ellie fluffed her scarf in my face and asked me again, her voice even more whispery this time. I was light-headed as we groped at each other under the restaurant's Formica table, our salads untouched in front of us, while everyone else seemed to be having joyless, plain lunches. I ran my hand up and down her stockinged leg; her fingers danced on my thighs. I thought I would explode, and felt my face flush. That afternoon we went back home, made love, got dressed again, and went back to work. Later, I thought I smelled of my wife's perfume and our sex, and alternately I was excited and deeply chilled by it.

I could always guess when Ellie was about to appear in front of me, asking me to come with her. At first this turn, her simple desire for me when I was feeling desperate, when everything had become so clouded, was strangely and strongly erotic. After lunch, after sex, Ellie was always in a talkative mood, but while her face was pink and soft, her words seemed to be coming from someone else.

Once, she spoke about a friend she decided she didn't like anymore, but gave no real reason. "I'm just not interested" is what she said when I tried to get her to explain why. Another afternoon, it was about a new client of hers. Ellie rolled her stocking slowly up her leg, and then stood to straighten my tie. "She accused me of eating some candy she had in a drawer," Ellie said, "and then leaving the wrappers on the table to taunt her. How's my hair?" she asked, looking in the mirror.

"Fine. Did you?"

"One piece. One little piece. Anyway, now she's working with Sally—at her request. And they can have each other as far as I'm concerned. Assholes."

But if I made some comment suggesting that she shouldn't have eaten the candy, or reminding her that Sally was a loyal friend, or hinting that she shouldn't call Moira at work so often—if I said what I wanted to say to her about her hardness, I'd begin to feel her moving away again. I knew that to anyone else, even to people we'd known forever, we still made an enviable pair. But if they looked closer, they'd see how tightly Ellie clung to me, when she used to roam by herself in her field of friends, catching my eye from time to time in a comforting way. My arm was stiff from supporting her, and from resisting the urge to push her away, and my throat was tight from not screaming at her to leave me alone. Her fingers dug into me and held me back until I ached as she whispered and told me things and wanted to believe that I understood.

One noon Ellie and I were eating in a restaurant down the block from her office, a place she'd chosen but I knew she didn't really like. Her foot slipped out of its shoe and rested on mine, and I dreaded it would be one of those afternoons. Ellie turned when a foursome of her colleagues came in, flooding the place with enthusiasm. They passed our table quickly, without saying hello, but gave me small sympathetic smiles. I faked a smile in return, but they had already turned away. Sally trailed in a minute behind them and threw back her head so that a large tail of hair flashed in the overhead light. Her eyes shifted for one second toward Ellie, and then quickly back to the others. I hated her for this. My wife's mouth tightened defensively.

"How come you don't spend time with them, with Sally, anymore?" I said, and glanced in their direction. "Or that new woman you met at your health club? What was her name? You said you liked her a lot. How come you don't call her?"

"That was over a year ago," she said, as though I should have known better. "I don't even remember her name." She took a bite of her sandwich. "Sounds like you don't want to have lunch with me. Is that what you're saying in your own way?"

I suddenly felt too tired for this again. "It isn't that I don't want to have lunch with you, it's that I don't want you to have lunch with *just* me. Really, how about *them,* for instance?" I tipped my head toward Sally's table again.

"Them," she tipped her head as I had, "they don't want to have lunch with me, isn't that obvious? Can't even bring themselves to say hello."

"Why should they? Jesus, Ellie, no one knows what to do with you anymore, not me, not Moira, your friends. Nobody knows how they're supposed to act around you, or what you want. You've turned everyone off, do you see that?"

"The problem really is," she said, "that you don't like things to change, do you? You would like me to be exactly as I've been for years, so you can be exactly as you've been and we can be just like we've always been too."

"Look, Ellie, people die. Pam died, but you still have to find a way to go on with your life and let me go on with mine. You have to make the good parts work for you—and for us. You have friends, people who really love you, who you can talk to, who can help."

"I talk to you now." Ellie stood up. "When you listen," she added, in the saddest voice I'd ever heard from her.

"That's not fair. I always listen to you, always," I said.

I paid the check and took my wife by the arm, but she pulled away and walked in front of me. She squinted at the sun and put on her sunglasses, and I knew that I had to follow her home then, this was part of our new routine. As she stood in front of me in our bedroom and undressed, her familiarity was suffocating.

"What you said at lunch? You're wrong about friends," she said, and unbuttoned my shirt. Her hands were cold on my chest, across my nipples. "They don't really love me in the way you imagine. Only you love me that way, and only I love you that way too. *You're* my friend, Jack."

I saw that this was true—she'd been showing me for months—and the concrete truth of our marriage. I'd always only had her—a man really only has his wife—but now I understood that she thought she really only had me. Ellie pulled me down on top of her, and passively I lay there. She covered my face with her hands, and then put her fingertips on my lips. As much as I wanted to make love to her—and I suppose that was the issue, desire for each other, hers and mine—I couldn't. She looked up at me, her thin arms pinned down by my hands. I knew that she was twisted painfully under me, but wouldn't tell me to stop. This urge to hurt her was like walking through a broken window, a danger-ous place to pass once, easier the second time around, and I didn't let up.

I felt a terrible panic then, that here in front of me was the rest of my life, that I would be with this woman forever, because I loved her, because this is what I would do certainly, because not being with her was never an option. It made me dizzy enough to put my head down and look through my naked bony knees that straddled her legs, past my penis that hung down over her. I saw the quilt bunched at the end of the bed, one of the countless things we'd liked together, bought together, because we'd always agreed on things. I saw my bare feet, veined and tufted with white hair already like an old man's. I knew that I was kneeling on the edge of something, the edge of my marriage, I suppose—or the beginning of the end, as they say—looking over a drop so sheer as to be unimaginable.

There's no way of knowing what a woman owns until she's dead. Until it's time to clean out her closets and drawers to make room for something else, there's no way of knowing what she needed, and wanted, to hide.

"I've been thinking," my sixty-three-year-old father said, "that it's time to go through your mother's things. You'll come over and see what you want." Although his call came on a day that had no particular significance I could think of—anniversary, birthday, end of the fiscal quarter—I wasn't particularly surprised, and in fact, I'd been uneasily anticipating it for a while.

For almost four years after my mother's death, my father didn't touch a thing, not because he'd be knocked over by some sort of sentimental, obvious grief, but because he hadn't figured out quite the best way to handle the situation. But in the space of six months, things had begun to change. Whatever the new life my father envisioned for himself actually entailed, I noticed that it meant getting rid of one of the twin beds from his bedroom and moving the remaining one to the center of the wall. His new life didn't require change, just slight adjustments. Pink silk pillows disappeared. The flowery soaps from the bathroom were replaced by white odorless bars. But the things that had been "theirs" for thirty-four years of marriage—paintings, a clock, kitchen knives, things that anyone could use—he allowed to stay.

If my father had removed everything that had openly been my mother's from the house, finally it meant he'd have to remove what was hidden as well. He was a man who hated anything not quite finished—an undercooked roast beef, a slowly dissolving marriage, a person who had not made up his mind—and the thought of his dead wife's high heels lined up and in boxes, of her coats on wooden hangers, of her handbags on the shelf, must have made him tense every time he walked by her closets.

I'd chosen a Sunday afternoon to go through my mother's belongings, a silver-blue day in January I wouldn't miss or re-member. I could see the back of my husband's head through my kitchen window as I sat in the driveway warming up the car. I will be quick, I thought, prudent, back soon. "This won't take long," my father said, helping me off with my coat. "Let me take that for you." I followed him up the stairs to his bedroom. He took each step slowly, and his hand strained on the banister, not out of fear or sadness, I knew, but out of age, something I hadn't noticed before.

"There are the two closets here," he said, tapping the door of each, "and two bureaus. I've put out some bags for you to put your mother's things in. Someone will be by next week to pick them up." Across his thin single bed, my father had laid out, side by side, green garbage bags. "I'll be downstairs," he said and left the room.

I sat on the edge of the bed and listened to my father take the long flight of stairs. Many times when I'd lived in his house, I'd listened in the same way, waiting for the last squeaky step to tell me it was okay to turn on the television again after I'd been told to keep it off, or jam a piece of candy in my mouth. And now that I was thirty-one I was still listening for that last step, and when my father finally reached it, I realized I was alone. I could look in my mother's closets and she'd never know, she'd never catch me.

I opened the closet door a few inches, tentative, as though something alive might rustle behind the clothes. I expected the air to be warm, breathlike, but it was slightly chilled, almost refrigerated, and it smelled of dust and old wool. I didn't know where to begin, so I began in the middle and pulled out whatever I happened to touch first.

I took dress after dress out of the closet and into the light, held each one up, appraising them quickly, but not really looking beyond the fronts and buttons and collars. Everything looked enormous, much bigger than my mother had been, as though by sitting in the closet her clothes had expanded and lost their shape like an old woman sitting in a soft armchair.

There were things of my mother's I'd never seen before, but I could tell by the yellowed necklines and oily armpits that they'd been worn many times. Certain dresses, stiff, with covered buttons and double pleats, reminded me of corners of the house, of particular foods and places to sit, of other people, of some particular time in my life, and of no time. On the floor in front of the closet, I made two piles: what I would keep, and what I would give away.

Some of the clothes felt dirty, as though they had been worn just last week. On others, lively lines of discoloration ran down the front of blouses and sweaters; splatters of something scrubbed but not removed spotted the hems of skirts and the sleeves of robes. My mother's clothes had always been perfect, as though she only wore them for minutes at a time, as though she didn't sweat and stain like everyone else. My own clothes had always been, and often still were, held together by safety pins, staples in the hem. I'd worn long sweaters to cover broken zippers, and vests to cover missing buttons, not because we couldn't afford to buy new things, but because I enjoyed hiding the small tears and careless stains from my mother, and she never looked beyond what I presented her. But now I saw clothes in her closet that were stained and imperfect, and she had kept them all. The pile I wanted to keep grew slowly, while the pile to give away spread out onto the floor as if it were trying to crawl away.

My mother had never allowed me to look in her closets. Once, when I was seven, I opened the door to one of them, and buried my face in the mother-smell of her dresses. In the dark, surrounded by her things, I didn't hear her come into the bedroom. She pulled me out by the shoulders, and out of surprise, or fear, or instinct, I held onto one of her dresses as though it would save me from being dragged out to sea.

"A woman deserves a little privacy," she said, removing the dress from my hand. "I don't go in your things, you don't go in mine."

I stood there, watching her put the dress back on the hanger, waiting for her to say something else. My eyes tingled from the light of the room after the black of the closet and I blinked at her. But she didn't say anything more, shut the door of the closet and left the bedroom, leaving me standing there. I listened to her go downstairs, and I wondered if she'd come up again if she heard the noise of her hangers banging together or her closet door opening. I could have opened her closet again, felt her things, teased her by waiting until she was all the way downstairs to rub her clothes, but I looked at the door she'd shut, and didn't touch it.

When I was older, there were nights my parents would go out and I would wander through their big house in almost darkness, tiptoeing through their living room and their dining room, touching their things. I would sit in the chair in my father's study and touch the knobs of his desk drawers, lean my elbows on his desk, and leave. I would stand with my back against the wall and watch a room in the dark, watch the leaf of a plant fall off by itself. I would lie on my mother's bed, stiff and straight, never comfortable because I thought she would come back any minute, and I'd look over toward my father's bed and think, this is what it's like to be married.

I wasn't allowed to use their bathroom. But when they were out, I'd sit on their toilet in the dark, unable and maybe not needing to pee, looking out the window onto the yard next door. As I sat there, I felt a draft around my ankles and thought, this is where my mother and father sit. I always flushed the toilet and stood there watching the bowl refill, twirling silver in the near dark, and waited to leave until everything was quiet again.

I was always afraid of being caught at something, or feeling a firm hand surprise my shoulder, of turning to face my mother and see my father moving behind, listening, but not joining. I knew I wouldn't be caught now, but the magnified sounds in the bedroom, the feeling of lightness in my body and tracelessness of my movements, were still there. I was comforted by the familiarity; I didn't want my mother back.

I took a white robe with red piping from the closet and held it up. I had only seen the robe once before, when my mother left the door of her bathroom open slightly. I looked in and saw her standing, one foot up on the sink, the other on the rug, shaving her legs. Between her thighs I saw hair, dark, deep, and unmotherly. The water in the bathtub behind her was running, and her head was lost in the steam. I went and sat in my room with the door shut, and wondered if my father had ever seen what I had just seen, and while I didn't want to think about it ever again, the picture kept reappearing to me, sometimes at dinner, sometimes with my eyes closed in bed, and I felt embarrassed for my mother. I had seen something she didn't know I'd seen.

I took the robe off the hanger and pressed it to my face for the smell. It was dusty like the other clothes, but it was still a brilliant white and red soft cotton, and I remembered how it had hung over the slope of my mother's back that day in the bathroom, the belt hanging down like a tail. I folded the robe and put it on my pile to keep.

I opened the drawers of her bureau. There were scarves, fluffy and coiled together, some invisibly crusty, that moved like stirring kittens. There were drawers of underwear. Slips and bras were adjusted and held together with safety pins and clasps, and several were torn at the lacy edges. My mother's underpants were all white, but now slightly yellowed, thrown into the drawer like important wads of paper. The waistbands crackled and dissolved when I stretched them. I wanted to take the drawer and dump the contents into one of the plastic bags like so much sand, and hit the sides to make sure the last piece fell out. I felt embarrassed suddenly, as though my mother were in the room, helplessly watching this invasion of her privacy, but I stuck my hand deep into the drawer among the coolness of her things, looking for something hard, unusual—not underwear.

Every woman I knew hid something in her underwear drawer, a place she was sure no one would ever want, or dare, to go. In my own drawer, I hid a letter from a man before my husband, a single earring I was afraid to lose, and a candy bar I didn't want to share. But my fingers wiggled around in my mother's underwear, as though I were going through the thickest head of hair, and didn't find anything that didn't feel like everything else.

My mother didn't walk around without her clothes on, never in a robe, never while dressing. I didn't sit on the edge of a bed and talk to her while she paced from drawer to closet to drawer deciding what to wear. Instead, I stood in the hall outside my parent's bedroom, listening to their low voices and the noises of dressing—a zipper going up, a shoe falling to the floor, my mother asking my father to button something. They appeared to me, every morning and every night, as fully dressed people. I never looked at myself in the mirror when I dressed. I never understood that it was easier to stand to pull on a pair of underpants than it was to sit and slide them up. To stand, to feel air run between my legs and across my chest felt too exposed, and too dangerous.

The second closet was full of my mother's shoes, handbags, and coats. Each shoe had a shoe tree stuck in it like a fist in an open mouth, and the pairs were lined up like soldiers' boots. A few years before she died, my mother had complained of back pain, and my father insisted she see a doctor. The doctor suggested she stop wearing high heels.

"I would appreciate it," my father said to me, "if you'd take your mother to get some new shoes. You'll pick her up and take her out for a few hours."

My mother sat tight-mouthed in the front seat of my car on the way to the shoe store. "I don't see what difference it will make," she said.

"What difference what will make?" I asked.

"Flat shoes. What difference flat shoes will make. They look so awful on a woman."

"I'm wearing flat shoes," I said, "and I'm very comfortable."

"I know you are," she said, "but comfort isn't everything." She did buy some flat shoes that day.

"I wouldn't have wanted you to spend all this time with me," she said on the way home, "and not have me buy anything."

She had trouble with her new shoes. After so many years of wearing high heels, her Achilles tendons had shortened, and she found it painful to walk. "I won't get used to this," she warned, and she stopped walking as much as she had before. It wasn't the pain, I thought, it was the look that made her sit down and hide her feet from view.

"It's very hard for a woman to have big feet like you do," she told me. "Men don't find it attractive. Your father loves women in high heels, but I guess some women just can't wear them."

I looked at my mother's shoes with their pointed heels and pointed toes, and realized that I never had, and never could, wear them. As I went through pair after pair, I saw that many of the toes were scuffed like my own shoes, that there was dirt and gum stuck to the bottoms, that the insides were dark from sweat. My mother thought the idea of wearing a pair of bowling shoes that someone else had worn right before was the most disgusting thing she'd every heard. Your odors, your decaying teeth, your scabs and earwax were to be looked at in private, never talked about with other people. I filled one garbage bag full of her shoes.

The handbags were lined up on the top shelf like books, perfectly aligned, the handles flopping in the same direction, ready to be grabbed and taken out. There were ostrich-skin bags that looked like they were covered with dried cat nipples, alligator bags, brown leather bags with gold clasps that closed like a kiss. I looked in each one for something—a note, the stub of a theater ticket, a pill, the odd things I imagined she kept in there—but each was clean, as though the bags were for rent only and not for keeps. My father bought my mother her pocketbooks, as she called them, and would return with one for her whenever he went on a trip. They would giggle together as she unwrapped the bag, and she would pull down his face to kiss his cheek. It seemed dirty to me—he was giving her that closed hard thing that always hung off her wrist, or in front of her crotch, or on her lap. She would open her bag very slightly and secretly, as though there was a bird inside she was afraid might fly out. Sometimes she left her bag in the kitchen, or on a table near the front door, and I would stroke the leather, put my hand only partway through the handles, and never look inside. I put all the handbags in a plastic garbage bag except for the ostrich-skin one.

I heard my father moving around downstairs and waited for him to come up. I didn't know how long I'd been going through my mother's things, and the light outside looked no different than when I'd arrived. My arms felt heavy from too much lifting, the inside of my nose dusty, my hands chapped. I felt no sadness for my mother, only a kind of tiredness at the predictability of everything I saw. She had hidden nothing, and had spent all those years trying to keep me away from something that didn't exist, while I had spent those years thinking there was something to find. My father stopped moving downstairs, and I could picture him sitting on the couch, legs crossed and looking toward the television, but really looking out the window, sensing there was something going on upstairs that he couldn't quite feel.

I had only my mother's coats left to go through. The garbage bags were filled and tied as though they contained years of leaves from the front yard. Some coats I tried on, but the sleeves revealed my wrists and the cloth pulled over my back. My mother had a coat for every occasion and weather, while I had just two—for cold and really cold. Out of all her coats, I decided to keep only the green one.

When I was fifteen, my mother saw me come in the front door from school, and she said, "That coat is horrible looking. You shouldn't put your hands in the pockets—it makes them sag. And your chest is getting too big for it."

"Why have pockets?" I asked. "I need to keep my hands warm."

"That's not what pockets are for," she said. "It's time to buy you a new coat."

We went to a department store that afternoon—she didn't even allow me to take off my coat first. She led me through the aisles and to the elevators with a purposefulness I saw in no one else. She didn't even talk to me, and I didn't know what to say to her.

In the coat section, I ran around the racks trying everything on, trying to get a response out of my mother. As I stood in front of the paneled mirror, I saw myself imposed on my mother, who stood behind me. I thought she hated the way I looked—I looked nothing like her.

"How about this one?" I said.

"Whatever you like," she answered, but I knew she wasn't really seeing me, that her head was turned toward another part of the store.

I was sweating and scratchy under my clothes as I tried on coat after coat. I felt that she had given up on me then, that it had taken all her energy to look and disapprove of me once, and now there was no point. I put on coats I knew she'd hate, and ones that were too expensive, but she continued to stand in one spot, her purse held down in front of her stomach. Finally, I saw a green coat like the one she was wearing.

"How about this one?" I said.

"That's nice," she said. "It's a good color on you."

She bought the coat, and as I watched the saleswoman wrap it in tissue and put it in a box, I knew I'd never like it. On the way home, with the box on my lap, I knew that the coat would always seem to belong to some other girl, and I'd end up treating it better than something I really liked.

"Show your father," my mother said when we got home.

I put the coat on, the tags hanging down like leaves.

"Very nice," my father said. "It looks like your mother's."

Now I put the coat in my pile, and decided that I might actually wear it sometime. People would say it was very unlike me.

I shut the closet doors and the drawers, and lined up the plastic bags in the hallway. The room looked exactly as it had before. The things I wanted to take fit easily into one bag, and I carried it downstairs.

My father was sitting in the living room as I had imagined, watching television in the dark.

"Mind if I turn on a light?" I said.

"Go ahead," he said, standing up the second I switched on a lamp. "All done?" He got up to meet me at the door of the room, blocking my way in. "Let me help you with your coat."

"I left the bags out in the hallway," I said, talking over my shoulder, as he guided me, one hand on my back, to the front hall. "I took some things."

"Good for you," he said. I looked at him, but his eyes were downward. "Thank you." When he opened the door for me, I leaned over and kissed him on the cheek. As though I'd done nothing, he stepped back and shut the door behind me.

The garbage bag full of my mother's clothes sat on the back seat of my car for several weeks, the plastic tearing and stretching as I pushed it around to make room, threw things on top of it, picked it up when it spilled to the floor after a fast stop. The clothes didn't come inside my house where I would have to talk about them, hang them in my closet. Instead, they froze at night in the back of the car on a dark street and warmed in the sun during the day. I used one of my mother's sweaters to clear away a fogged windshield and saw the water bead up on the wool that had once touched her chest.

Only the bathrobe came inside, and I washed it by hand in the sink. I was naked underneath when I wore it, and I lay down on my bed, flat and straight, and when I heard my husband coming toward the room, I took it off and threw it in a corner of the closet.

Driving on a Sunday afternoon, I smelled the clothes baking in the sun on the back seat. They looked dirty now, and faded in the light of the snow. I drove to a part of the city that was quiet. Few people were out, and I couldn't see faces, as people stared out of the wind. I looked down the street and saw the traffic lights swinging together, blinking and fading until they were smoky and blurred.

At the storefront Goodwill, there was a small crowd, bent and busy. When I pulled the car up next to the curb, I could see that the drop-off itself was shut, but boxes, bags, and piles of clothing crowded the doorway and spilled out onto the sidewalk, coloring the concrete. The people, some in pairs, one black, some white, one Chinese, dug into the boxes as though there was warmth at the bottom.

I hadn't expected anyone to be there watching as I left my mother's clothes. I sat in the car, the heat roaring, unable to jump out and dump the stuff. Occasionally, people pulled something out of a box or a bag and held the sweater or the skirt or the pants in front of themselves, smoothing the clothing across the bulki-ness of their coated bodies, modeling to their partners, or watch-ing themselves in the window next door. They checked labels, inspected seams, held the clothes up to smell them, and what they liked they folded and smoothed and placed in bags by their sides.

In a few minutes the crowd had gone, and there was just one man in a red down jacket and wool hat, rummaging in the piles that others had already been through. He extracted single socks and a pair of boots. When he was finished, he picked up his two bags and walked down the street and around the corner.

I got out of the car quickly, reached into the back seat, and dragged out the bag of my mother's clothes. The plastic was breaking, and by the time I'd carried it to the doorway, things had spilled behind me, leaving a trail to my car. I ran to pick them up and threw them back on the pile.

I didn't drive away. I sat there for a few minutes, rubbing my hands to warm them, sweating, slightly scared and a little excited to see what might happen. The Chinese couple came back again, as if they'd been watching from a window for new arrivals. The woman handed the man her bags, and he stood back as she picked up a blue blouse of my mother's, elegant and thin, and held it in front of her plaid coat. Her friend nodded once, she folded it, and they left again.

Then the man in the red down jacket came back. Looking around to make sure he was alone, and seeing no one, he began to dig through the pile. I saw his gray face turn in my direction and not see me. He held up one of my mother's slips, turned it around and around as though he were twirling a dancer, looked inside, and dropped it back on the pile.

And then I was guilty and hearing my own quick breath as he held up my mother's sweaters and checked the seams and the labels, and I wondered what made him drop them back on the pile. He held up a summer dress, one that had concealed zippers and a fine line of embroidery. It flapped like a flag, and he rolled it up and stuffed it in his bag. He picked up the ostrich-skin purse. Holding it close to his chest, he looked around again and then opened it very slightly. He stuck his hand inside and found nothing. A cough, shaky and wet from deep inside me, found its way out—he'd found nothing more than I had. When the man crouched on his heels, his jacket pulled up and his pants pulled down, and I could see his crack exposed to the cold. He held up my mother's green coat that I had never brought inside my own house, never even tried on, examined it with expert eyes, and with his free hand, hiked up his pants.

He checked the pockets of the coat and turned them inside out, he opened the coat and checked the lining, and when he stuck his gloved hand up the sleeve, it seemed that he was doing something violent and rude to my mother, and I felt a red shame crawl up my face. The man looked around again, and still seeing no one, took off his own red jacket and put on the green coat. He twirled in it, and looked down his front. The coat was small and hugged him tightly, and the too-short sleeves showed his hairy wrists. He managed to button the middle button by hiking the long part of the coat around his waist like a skirt. Then he put his red jacket over the green coat and picked up his bags. As he walked down the street, I saw the bottom of my mother's green coat flapping behind him like the tail feathers of a bird.

CLAUDE COMES AND GOES

You wouldn't think I'd be sad to see my wife's old lover go, especially after what I saw tonight, but I am, really much sadder than you can imagine. I'm not sure either of us, my wife or myself, will ever see the man again. I might even use the word "lovely" to describe Claude tonight as I watch him walk away, not a word I generally think of when I think of a man, but it's not only how I see him in the flesh but also how he comes to mind at any random or bored moment, as though he's dead and I'm remembering him. I already know he's gone in a way.

Tonight I waited until the last moment to shut the front door—that is, until I could no longer see him, because he'd turned the corner at the end of our street to make his way to his apartment where he lives alone. The man doesn't even own a frying pan—I checked one night—because he eats out every meal. I've seen him hunched over a book and a plate in a restaurant that I sometimes pass on my way home from work. I hurry past, feeling sad for him, and when he's not there, he's eating with us. I know the way Claude cuts his meat like my grandmother did, timid and ineffectual, doesn't like many vegetables, picks the spongy middle of French bread.

But it's not only the way he eats. I know these evenings he's spent with us from the way he's made my wife laugh and lean back so far back in her chair that the front legs lift off the floor; made my own heart pound in my chest as though I were a teenager; made us, my wife and me, both feel that if we didn't think about it too much we could actually convince ourselves this was the time in our lives before children, before annoying jobs and bad houses, before people our own age got sick and had pieces cut out of them, before decisions that were made could not be unmade. This could be the time when we stayed up late and didn't clean up afterward, when broken appliances—the answering machine we suddenly can't live without, for instance, for even a day—stayed that way. This could be an altogether different time in our lives.

Tonight, after Claude left and I returned to the kitchen, my wife was bent over the dishwasher, a round back and firm behind in cotton pants facing me.

"Is he gone?" she asked, her voice muffled by her own body and by the cave of the machine.

"Gone," I said. I shut another door, this time the one in the kitchen that led out to the screened porch where we ate our meals in the warm weather, where we'd just eaten that night with Claude and stayed up drinking and laughing too loudly at his stories, many of which had him in the role of villain or cocksman. During one story, Nan had even reached over for my napkin to wipe her eyes. Her face was puffy from laughing and self-conscious enjoyment. And now it was almost midnight—Claude time, we called it, those of us who had always turned the lights out by ten—and I was tired. The crickets felt like a headache without the pain—someone else's, I suppose.

"Jesus, Martin," Nan said, standing up, her hands on her back to straighten her stiff spine. "Don't be so lazy. I haven't even cleared the table out there yet."

When I looked at her I saw that she was remarkably pale, her face the color of the gray hair that now mostly framed her round face. Only the curls on the top of her head remained their youthful brown—age had not yet risen that high. Her eyes widened as though something surprising was taking place in her fifty-five-year-old body, an internal uprising.

"Nan, what's the matter?" I said, holding onto her wrist.

"Nothing, I just stood up too fast, I guess. The blood drained or something."

Sure, I thought, that's all, pale through mere natural physiology, not like me, pale with sadness and a sudden feeling that I was stupefyingly dull—the dullest advertising executive, friend, husband, father ever. I know something my wife doesn't think I know, about all of us. Understand that her lying to me tonight is not painful.

"Do you realize," Nan said, coming back from the porch with her hands full of dirty glasses, "that we might never see him again? And we still have to pack."

That can't make sense to you, but I knew what she meant. Claude was dying "from the balls up," as he described it, tracing the line of malignancy that he imagined ran from his prostate to his brain.

The way he had drawn his cancer made me think of an army of ants I'd seen dragging crumbs in a straight line across the cool blue of a slate walk that morning.

"Figures it would get me where it counts," Claude had said, pointing to his lap. "Take my brain, take my eyes, just leave me this."

But tonight, months after we'd first heard he was dying, Claude looked even thinner and yellower than the last time we'd seen him—only three nights earlier—and we are going to Paris in the morning, leaving the house in just six hours to go to our son's wedding. I know that when we come back to our house the plants will be overgrown from a summer's month of neglect, the water still dripping in the bathroom sink, and Claude will probably be dead. I'll miss him, I know, miss what he does for my wife, what he does for us.

Nan and I were never the kind of people to put off packing until the last hour, take a cab to the airport vaguely hungover and exhausted. It's tough really to think about, this change, this lovely change in us over so soon. It makes my throat hurt, blocks it up so I can't cry.

"I'm going to water the plants," I said to my wife.

"At this hour? What about packing?"

"I'll do it later, I promise. Have you ever known me to keep you waiting? Have we ever missed a plane because I wasn't ready?" I snapped at her. "In thirty years of marriage, has this ever happened?"

Nan squeezed the remaining water from the sponge, shook her head sadly, as though she really would have liked to say, "Yes, you have done all those things at least once in all these years of marriage, and thank God for that, you're normal and sometimes I don't like you very much, but I'll always love you."

Like I said, I felt very dull then, but I'm not sentimental. I know that sometimes, at these times, you can confuse dullness with sadness, you can't tell the two apart. I brought one more load of dishes in from the porch and then went out to the garden. Nan headed up the stairs to our bedroom.

This bush, the one with those little cups of white flowers, the one that attracts bugs, this one I hold the hose to, drowning its roots. This was for me my burning bush, I could always say later, and it needed to be doused. The water soaked through the tip of my right sneaker as I looked up to see Nan moving around in our bedroom on the second floor, packing, and probably packing for me too, this woman intimate with my underwear and socks. I once saw her remove a hair from my toothbrush. I saw her clean up my vomit on the floor one night when I'd been sick, as though I were one of our sons, expectant, inarticulate, acid-mouthed but grateful. I couldn't think of what I hadn't seen her do really, when I put my mind to it. Of course, you see a lot you don't like to mention in thirty-six years—it's private, what we do for one another. We'd hide ourselves in shame if we were caught doing loving tasks, so much more than what we'd do for ourselves.

More water on a drowning bush. Claude showed up almost

nine months ago, single again for the third time, nothing his lat-est ex-wife had done too private to mention. I had never met the man, Nan had not seen him in almost twenty years, but we heard about him, read his byline in the New York paper where he was a theater critic, saw his picture in magazine pages with his latest (now ex) wife, stunningly beautiful and stunningly taller than this little elf-like man whose one-quarter Japanese heritage showed in his face, as though it were many times stronger than whatever else was there. He was flamboyant in a way we envied—attractive and lively, like a little beetle.

The first night Claude came over to our house, we sat stiffly in the living room—I even had on a blazer and real shoes, and Nan had put on some makeup—being hosts, flattered by his presence, this famous man other people talked about and listened to. He seemed exotic to me—big city liver, big name, a mysterious an-cestry. We passed the peanuts, I filled Claude's drink, until I real-ized he'd rather do it himself. At dinner, Nan and I were shocked by his stories, maybe amused too. Her foot tickled mine under the table.

"Get this," it said. "He uses the word 'pussy' like I use garlic."

"She douched after sex," Claude said, eating away at the heav-ily spiced meal Nan had cooked in honor of his visit. "Married to the woman for fourteen years and she still felt she had to clean herself up after sex. Former actress, hygiene freak. She used to punish the kids if they farted in public. I think what bothered her most about my sleeping with other women was that I came home dirty, not that I was unfaithful."

"That's just symbolic," Nan said. "Washing herself was a ges-ture, not a thing in itself."

I had to admit to Nan later in the dark when she couldn't see my face—I felt as young as a twenty-six-year-old—that I felt uncomfortable about the conversation. She'd slept with Claude years before we were married. He'd been her first; she'd been one of thousands, probably. Nan, fresh out of college with beautiful breasts and high academic ambition, had fallen in love with this man her size, a man who took her to clubs and made her dance until her feet swelled. They drank drinks no one orders anymore, she smoked cigarettes, and I was there too. Not that I ever saw them or knew who they were, but I did the same thing in those days, danced and smoked and thought I was pretty wonderful. She says that she knew she wouldn't last by Claude's side—he was moving on to great things and he didn't take women with him. He only found them when he got there. Okay by her, she'd explained.

"I was in love with him," she'd said, in response to me, her timing perfect as she slipped in naked next to me in bed and stuck her foot between my legs, high up. "Every girl was. I can't even remember what making love with him was like. He's really more an old friend, I think, not a lover—I have no feelings for him that way. Besides, I'm sure this is the last time we'll see him. He had to call us, you know? New in town? Lonely? We're way too dull for him. He'll hook up to some fast crowd and that will be that. Consider it a courtesy call."

I asked my wife to move her foot back and forth a little. Tomorrow was a work day, me back to the agency—responsible me, the eponymous founder of this big-billing machine, Nan back to her office and students at Wellesley. That was that—her foot stayed there, we slept.

Claude called two nights later while Nan was away at a conference on Women and the Renaissance.

"Martin," he said, "you weren't asleep or anything, were you?"

"Not at all," I said—nine-thirty—tired, not asleep, "but Nan's out of town."

"I want you, Martin," Claude laughed. "I need a man tonight."

"What can I do for you, Claude?" He made me uncomfortable. I chose to be straight, my business voice.

"Look, I managed to drag this armchair up two flights of stairs to my apartment, but it's stuck on the landing. Can't move it, can't leave it there. I need you to give it a push."

"Now?" It was impossible not to wonder why he was moving

a chair at nine-thirty, but I didn't ask. It was the kind of question I might have asked one of my sons, provoking in him that eternal adolescent exasperation.

"Listen, I can't leave it here. It's blocking someone's door. They'll try to get out tomorrow and find they can't. They'll be late for work, lose their job, their marriage will go to hell, and they'll kill themselves. You want that on your conscience?"

"No back stairway, I take it," I said.

I put down my book, got dressed again, having already changed out of my clothes right after dinner, and walked to Claude's apartment. He was sitting on the front steps, alert like a kid on a city stoop, and together we pushed the chair up to the apartment. His muscles were stringy, but he was amazingly strong for someone so mouse-like.

"Have a drink," he said, moving into the galley kitchen. "Gotta find some glasses."

Everything was white, and the place had no shades. The bedroom had a bed, beautiful and antique, unmade—never made, I imagined—and clothes spilling out of boxes. Claude was teaching drama criticism at Harvard for the year, and books and student papers were towered in the living room.

He handed me a coffee mug full of scotch.

"My kids," he said, seeing me look at the only picture in the place, a black and white photograph in a delicate gold frame. "The twins, Michele and Daniel."

"How old?"

"Thirteen. Beautiful. I miss them. Sit."

"On what?" I asked.

"The floor, Martin." Already he'd piled the chair we'd dragged in with books and papers, a hasty attempt to clean. Nan liked clean surfaces, stuff hidden and messy in closets was okay, but flat expanses should be kept that way. I felt a sudden pang of envy when I saw a pair of dirty socks resting comfortably in the corner. It had been so long since the thought of doing something like that—leaving my things where they fell—had even occurred to me, I wondered if it ever had. I wondered what I had once liked, leaned to.

Already—fifteen minutes there, but I'm an intuitive man, it's my business—I could feel there was something desperate about Claude, some need that made me feel slightly concerned. Sometimes you recognize this in a person, but you can walk away. It's like seeing a fat man, all alone at a party, stuff himself at the hors d'oeuvres table. You just turn around, saddened for a second at most.

"How's the big H treating you?" I asked.

"Harvard? Fine. Students aren't all so bright, but that hardly matters anymore these days. Who needs brains to watch a Gurney play?"

"Gurney? Nan and I loved his play we saw last year."

Claude got up to pee for the second time that night, and for the second time, left the door open.

"Shit, Martin," he yelled over his shoulder. "You couldn't have. I have a lot to teach you. At least Nan used to have good taste. Don't know you well enough to say the same about you." Claude faced me as he zipped up his pants.

I smiled and lay back on the floor. I would like to be taught, educated in this different life. Claude talked and the scotch knotted in my chest. He asked me about my job—fascinated by the fact that the Burger King account was mine, about my boys, two of them, grown up and far away, about my garden which I loved and suddenly felt prissy about, what Nan and I did for vacations, who did the laundry, the cooking, what it was like to own a house, to make lots of good money. All the time, he sat cross-legged on the floor, almost an alien from another planet, asking, "Tell me, how do you do it where you come from? Educate me, teach me."

Claude told me about some of the women he'd slept with—he had shared a midtown Manhattan apartment with a friend for sex purposes, trading off the afternoons—not in a crude or boastful way, but as a matter of fact. It was part of his life—just like

I'd told him I'd grown big-boy tomatoes last year instead of beef-steaks. It's a matter of taste, I'd explained, of fullness and color. I'd used my hands as though I were cupping a woman's ass.

I couldn't counter with stories of my own infidelity—there were none—and he didn't expect them. I think it would have made him cry, this picture of me and Nan, and our life shattered, made as jagged as his. Nan was no longer a former girlfriend of his, she was my wife, sacred, and it hardly seemed that he had known her, known her in any way other than as my wife. Claude spoke about his work in a language reserved for people who care about the theater. He mentioned that he'd always wanted to learn how to cook and garden. Maybe this year he'd take some classes, maybe meet some women, he said, winking and sipping.

"Maybe I'll slow down," he said. "What do you think, Martin? Should I do that?"

I nodded, his question seemed genuine. I knew this man wanted to be friends with me. He seemed starved for it—he had no real friends, I guessed, and never would. I remembered back, years before, the way I marveled at how my eldest son, John, made friends so easily in the playground. One offer of a shovel, one invitation to look at a dead bird under the bush, one inquiry, and he was hooked. Claude hooked me.

When I finally got up to leave at one-thirty, I could see in Claude's eyes that he liked me, admired me even. What a boost, what fun, how unusual. I'm a much bigger man than Claude, and I felt a little awkward shaking his hand, so I touched him on the shoulder and he touched me on the back.

"Come see us soon," I yelled up the stairs on my way out. I meant it. "I mean it. Nan would enjoy it too."

"I will," he shouted back. "Very soon."

When I got home, the phone was ringing.

"Where have you been?" It was Nan, frantic in New Haven. "I've been trying you since ten."

"Claude's. I helped him move a chair. We had a drink."

There was a pause. "Was it . . . ?" she said, at a loss for words. "What was it like? He invited you?"

"Yes, he called. It was great. He's a lot of fun."

"Martin, it's almost two. Don't you have to work tomorrow?" It almost sounded like she was scolding me.

"Of course. So what?"

"Nothing, just checking. I'll see you around dinnertime. I want to hear everything about tonight. Really? You were at Claude's? What's his place like? Forget it, tell me tomorrow. I love you, Martin." That to cover a hint of jealousy.

"I love you," I said. We hung up, and I got into bed. The house creaked and settled as I did. I was alone that night, very much like Claude, probably as close to being like him as I'd ever come. I missed my big boys and wondered what it must be like to lose your children at thirteen, when mustaches are sprouting and breasts are budding and everything is mixed up inside one crazy, lovable child's mind. I never admitted to Nan that I adored the fury of my sons' adolescence. That's like admitting you like to watch violence in the street.

Several evenings later, I came home from work to find Nan and Claude in the kitchen. He was dressed in black pants and an olive-green linen shirt, tastefully wrinkled, leaning against a counter while she cooked, his legs crossed at the ankles. Immediately, I loosened my tie as I walked in on their laughter. I was some television bread-winning type still lugging a briefcase, tassels on my shoes, slight indigestion, a nasty day at the office.

"Martin," Claude said hurriedly, "I remembered you said you liked fish, and I saw some of this gravlax today and thought of you."

A pink slab, like an exposed triangle of female flesh, lay on a plate which he offered me. I had to put down my briefcase to accept it.

"He came by to give it to you, and I thought he could have dinner with us," Nan said, wiping her hands on her apron to give me a kiss. "There's plenty."

"Great, sounds good. Give me a minute." I went upstairs to change my clothes—I felt like Mr. Rogers trying to look casual—and heard them laughing again in the kitchen.

"Nan says I should help you pick some herbs for the meat," Claude said, meeting me at the bottom of the stairs. He followed me out to the garden. He was as quiet as a child wanting to please, watching me pinch the basil leaves at just the right spot.

"Like this?" he said, but his pinch was clumsy; it pulled the plant. He was too busy watching my face for something to see what he was doing. His fingers moved without grace.

"Just like that," I said. He beamed, he blushed a mustard yellow, he carried the leaves in his hand inside to Nan. He offered them to her, and she smiled. It could have been a baby bird nesting there, the way he slowly unfolded his fingers to reveal the curling leaves in his palm.

It wasn't so many nights later, back at our house for dinner, that he made my wife cry. He'd showed up again, unannounced, this time bearing a dozen fresh bagels he'd brought back from his weekend trip to New York. His gift was his entrance, his hands full of generosity.

"God, I thought she was the smartest woman I'd ever met," Claude said about Nan while we ate dinner, but looking at me. We'd been talking about when they had first known each other. "Here was this beautiful girl with such a mind. I knew she was going to do some serious things, go to graduate school, write books, all too much and too smart for me. I was kind of scared of her, to tell the truth."

"That's ridiculous," Nan said. "You never seemed impressed. You said I should try acting or something, something completely unrealistic for me. I thought that showed a certain lack of respect."

"I was a shit then—still am, I suppose. Maybe I was trying to throw you off, you were so serious about things. I found myself having to think about some of the things you said because I didn't understand them at first. Your ideas were too complicated for me. I didn't want you to get so far ahead of me."

Nan, overburdened and distracted by the small and frustrating duties of her work—fighting with the stubborn teaching assistants and stupid students—began to cry at the table. Her own work—her field is early feminism—had been shelved for too long. I remembered this ambition too, this great brain slowed, the razor edge taken off by two children, maybe some bad choices, marriage to me. She didn't complain usually, and when she did, she blamed only herself, but I knew she thought things could have gone other ways. She always spoke for herself during these conversations—she wanted no advice or solace from me.

"This is ridiculous," she said, wiping her tears. "What am I crying for? Why am I upset? I'm going to get dessert."

When Nan left the table and went into the kitchen, Claude looked at me with such confusion, I had to reassure him.

"She's okay," I said, aching for my wife's disappointment. "Sometimes she feels bad about her work, that she hasn't done enough."

"I'm really sorry, Martin," he said. "I feel terrible. I didn't mean to make her cry. I meant just the opposite. Everything I said was true. You should have seen her back then, and now you two have everything, you've made the good, smart choices that I couldn't. How I envy you, really, Martin. I hope Nan understands."

Claude apologized to Nan when she came back into the room, and she smiled charmingly at him. I hadn't evoked anything like that in her in years, the tears or the smile of gratitude, not that our marriage was lacking its own intensity, just these unexpected jags that make knowing one another a slightly scary delight.

Claude cheered us up with a story of how he'd dated a very fat stage actress once.

"Fat as a whale," he said. "We went one night to this very *in* place where all the theater people were going and she squeezed herself into this tiny chair. The table cut into her stomach, and every time she laughed—she thought I was hysterical, and I made her laugh on purpose just to see the results—the table would rock, the wine would spill, the antipasto would slip, and she'd giggle and use her finger to clean it up. I couldn't let her on top of me, you understand. I wouldn't be here to tell the story."

He had us laughing again as he described making love to the woman in a too-soft bed until more tears ran down our cheeks—the ups and downs of another person's sex life ease our own tensions. Nan even snorted and then laughed at herself.

At night after he left, Nan and I would talk together, pumped up and excited about our luck at having Claude in our lives, and I silently felt a special blessing bestowed upon me in the form of my wife that I hadn't felt in years. While there would always be something proprietary about Nan's relationship to Claude—she'd known him first and longest—it was clear to both of us that he focused more on me, that he looked up to me. He liked my normalcy, I guess, my steadiness, my ability to do one thing for so long—all things I never much liked in myself. I can't say he made me feel differently about this, but I admitted his admiration. Still, left over from that night I'd sat in his apartment after having moved the chair up the stairs, was an uneasy feeling that he wanted something from me, that somehow I'd end up disappointing him only because I wasn't really sure what he wanted.

I was right, after all. Claude had something to tell us, he needed something from us.

"You know why I'm here, you two? In Cambridge?" he asked one night at dinner.

"The job," Nan offered.

"Free dinners?" I suggested. "No ex-wife?"

"All of the above, and more," he said. "How can I put this gracefully? I'm dying. Dying from the balls up." And that's when he traced the line from his crotch to his brain. Nan stopped, spoon in midair.

"What?" I asked. "What are you talking about?"

"Prostate, Martin. Watch out for your balls. Mine are rotten and rot spreads, if you know what I mean. They have some good docs in this town. I'm seeing the biggest of big specialists at MGH. Nan, don't look like that. It could be years you'll be stuck eating dinner with me. And look at it this way, I won't have to floss anymore," he said a smirk and then a giggle. Nan had lowered her head and I took a sip of wine. It wasn't that I didn't think he should laugh at his own horror, but how was I supposed to respond? Women have an easier time of it—their faces show natural sorrow easily.

"Don't you think it's fitting that this is where it should all start?" Claude pointed to his lap. "Sort of ironic, isn't it? Reminds me of that great golfer who got cancer in his hand. Where else could he get it?"

"Oh Claude," Nan sighed. "What can we do?"

"One more reason I'm here. I have a daughter at Harvard," he said looking down, this piece of news obviously more difficult to announce than the first. "She's a junior—nineteen years old. I had an affair with her mother so many years ago, and here she is, daughter of mysterious strangers. She knows who I am, always has, but I've never seen her. I've wanted to; she's my daughter, after all. I thought we could spend some time together this year— before I croak, at least. She knows I'm here, but I haven't called her yet."

Nan pressed her hand to her chest. "Oh, Claude, Claude, call her. She'll want to know. She'll want to know you."

"I'm not so sure," he said. "Did you ever notice it's easier to seduce a woman than to call one on the phone?"

"Let us know what we can do," I said. "Let us know how we can help you."

I poured him another drink, and it was after one when he finally left.

"We'll have to help him" was all Nan said before she rolled over in bed. "Who else will?"

I stared at the ceiling, my hand holding my balls, the mysterious source of trouble. No child of mine was walking around unclaimed, the result of some forgettable night. How would a man feel about such a thing? Everything I'd done was accounted for. Was that better? Had I made better choices than Claude? At least everyone I loved was where I knew they were.

For months I'd come home from work and find Claude in the

house, maybe alone if Nan had gone out for a few minutes or was still at her office. She would never admit that it was Claude—that night he'd made her cry—who had convinced her to change the way she worked, to go back to what she really liked, to cut out some of the other things. I was working not as hard suddenly, home earlier, relaxing more. I felt less oppressively responsible all the time. Claude would be reading a magazine in the living room, washing dishes left over from breakfast. Several times I found him in my garden pulling weeds and stacking them in tiny piles, dirt under his fingernails. He followed me; he followed me to the hardware store on a Saturday, showed up one morning at my office to say hello, looking pale and dizzy. He cooked with Nan, he took showers at our house when the water in his apartment was shut off. We had hilarious dinners together, full of spitting and spilling, squeals of pleasure, my own face tired from laughing. Silly stuff. It seemed that the three of us had always been doing this.

I heard him vomit in our bathroom, retching and the water running, I saw the yellow around his dark eyes. His arm was pocked from needle marks. I picked him up from a doctor's appointment one day and brought him to our house, put him in the boys' room, covered him with a quilt, and watched him shiver, watched the sweat collect above his lip and on his forehead. I wiped his chin later when he drooled some of the hot soup I'd made him. He seemed to have only us to take care of him, to love him. It never seemed we were losing.

Nan and I whispered outside his door about his temperature and about the odd color of his skin. She held my forearm and had that exasperated look on her face I remembered from when both boys had chicken pox at the same time—concern and frustration together. We watched in later weeks as Claude picked at his food; he seemed only to want to sit and be amused, and after he'd left (sometimes I drove him the fifteen blocks home), Nan and I could hardly bring ourselves to talk about what we were watching. I couldn't tell you how she felt, this woman I knew so well. We talked together—a sign that we had an indescribable, unalterable closeness—but I didn't press her for what I couldn't understand. Neither of us wanted to lose him now, but I wondered why we couldn't say that out loud. Did it make life before seem less than we thought it was?

And then in March, Claude felt much better. It was as though one day he'd simply regained a new spirit. He still looked worn out, but his mind was no longer so slow, and once again we all laughed together. Claude's daughter had not been mentioned since the first time he'd told us about her, but now with the color back in his face (he was dating a woman—a graduate student in one of his classes—and it made his eyes bright and darting) he decided that it was time to call Doria, the daughter he'd never met. He felt presentable again, his old and real self.

"I was wondering," he said one evening as he leaned against the counter in our kitchen, "if I could bring Doria over here some night. I can't cook for her myself—I don't even own a pan or really know how to make anything—and I don't want to take her out. That seems kind of impersonal. And I thought it would be nice if we all met."

Behind the easy request there was a look of terror in his eyes, pure fear and begging: don't leave me to do this alone.

"We'd love to," I said, now used to moving around him in the kitchen. It was like having one of our sons back. "Anytime really, right, Nan?"

"Just let us know," she said cheerfully. "We'd be delighted. We'd love to meet your daughter."

The dinner was scheduled for a Saturday evening, and Claude came over in the early afternoon to pace around the kitchen and ask if we needed help. He fidgeted with his clothes—he wore a jacket for the occasion—he dropped a plate on the floor, he coughed a little too much until Nan sent him into the other room to watch television. When I looked in around five-thirty, he had fallen asleep, his thin arm cocked over his eyes, his chest rising a little too fast for my comfort.

"Is he all right?" I whispered to Nan, whom I'd brought to the doorway to look at our sleeping friend.

She shrugged. "Let's get dressed." Upstairs, we changed clothes, nervous and silent with each other.

Doria was forty minutes late. I paced; Nan shook her head in the kitchen ("Don't you think it's rude?" she asked me), while Claude peered out the window in the front hall, kneeling on an old bench the cat used to sleep on, parting the curtain only a little bit to watch the street. When Doria finally arrived, I heard an awkward rhythm of voices in the front hallway, her voice lower and more sullen than his. He was chattering on in a way I didn't recognize. Claude brought his daughter into the kitchen to meet us. Nan and I pretended to busy our hands with the salad.

Father and daughter stood side by side. Doria was a beautiful girl, but there was something slightly morose about the way she hunched, the way her hair hung over her face. She looked much like Claude, same size and shape, with his coloring and exotic blood, but she never once smiled—he had a proud smile across his face that was in such contrast to hers—and shuffled her feet in heavy boots. She was dressed in black, her arms weighted by silver bangles, her face by embarrassment and discomfort. Claude hopped around, compensating for her; he steered her here and there, offering things to eat, drink, information. I could see that my wife, whose look was as patient and composed as ever, was annoyed with Doria. First, she would want to straighten the girl's back by pulling on her thin shoulders, then wipe her hair from her face, then say, "This is your father, for God's sake, act well. You are not a child." I stood and smiled, steady, a bolster for them all, and myself.

Sometimes silence is made worse by noise, which is what was happening as Claude attempted to fill the empty spaces by complimenting the food and asking his daughter questions she'd already answered. Nan is a less patient person than I am with the miseries and discomforts of people our kids' age, and she scowled through much of dinner. I tried to draw Doria out, to get her to engage with her father, who looked so desperate for something from her, even a scrap.

"Are you interested in the theater at all?" I asked Doria. "Your father knows just about everyone and everything worth knowing." Claude gave me a little nod, a small thanks.

"Not really," she mumbled. "I mean, I'm not that interested."

"Maybe later," I smiled at her. "Do you think you might take some theater courses next year?"

"Martin, I didn't like theater when I was her age either," Claude said. Doria didn't even look up at her instant ally, her instant father. "Too many really interesting things going on." If the comment was not directly pointed at her, Doria did not respond.

Again, the silences were too loud and I could almost hear our chewing, four mouths, eyes down, at one table. Maybe it was just my chewing I heard, my mind open to it, empty for something to say. The girl was difficult.

"May I have some more chicken?" Doria asked, holding her plate out to my wife.

"Certainly," Nan said, serving her. "Glad you like it."

"A good appetite," Claude said. "That's wonderful."

I felt pained for all of us. Nan studied Doria. She had always wanted daughters, not sons, even though she loved our boys completely, and I was wondering if Nan was thinking that this girl could have been her daughter, maybe Claude's and hers. And suddenly I was the odd person out at this odd gathering—not father, not husband, not lover of someone, just a man in this constellation by chance. The drama belonged to those other people: Nan for what she hadn't done and chosen, Claude for what he had done and walked away from, and Doria for what had been done to her.

Claude stopped eating and stared at Doria with wide moist eyes and utter love while she seemed not to notice. When Claude caught my eye, I raised my glass to him. I'm not sure why I did it, and even then I knew it was a gesture out of place, but Claude seemed buoyed by it, by the support, the push ahead.

"Martin has the most beautiful garden," Claude said. "Would you like to see it after dinner? Okay by you, Martin?"

"Please, be my guests, although it's a little early in the season. You'll have to come back when it's in full bloom, Doria."

"That's okay," Doria said, looking down. When she spilled a glass of wine across the tablecloth—I hadn't even seen her move—Nan pushed back her chair a little too loudly and left to get a sponge.

"It's fine," her father whispered to her gently. "Don't worry about it." His affection was as intense as her unease.

At nine the doorbell rang. Nan and I looked at each other—we were never the type to receive surprise visitors until Claude came around, and he was no longer a surprise, and hardly even a visitor.

"It's probably for me," Doria said, and so I walked with her to the front where a young man stood on the porch.

"My boyfriend," she said to me, and I opened the door. They kissed and whispered before I was introduced to Mark. He had a pleasant enough face. Both Nan and Claude jumped up when he came into the room.

"Would you like some dessert?" Nan asked. "We were just in the middle."

"Sure," Mark said, only slightly less sullen than Doria, whose face was softer than before as she leaned into him. She seemed almost to be hiding behind his wide shoulders.

Claude was now quiet and sharp, his mouth tight and downward. He refused to look at Mark or his daughter and told a story with a nasty, misogynist ending. I was sad to see so sudden a change in him—it seemed to lack strength. But I felt sorry for Doria. Why was she supposed to love this man? Who was he to her really?

Doria and Mark left while we were still having coffee, some whispered plan having been set between them, Mark's watch consulted several times. Claude and Nan remained at the table while I walked the others out.

"Saturday night," I said when I returned to the dining room. "Can't expect the kids to hang out with us all night."

"We're still drinking our coffee, Martin. It's not that late. They could have waited," Nan said, and then got up to take her cup into the kitchen.

I was left alone with Claude, and then there was really nothing to say except "disaster," or "total failure," or "I'm sorry, Claude," but I said nothing.

"I should go too," Claude said. "But thanks for dinner, thanks for doing it. I'm sorry it wasn't more pleasant. I'll see you soon." He leaned into the kitchen to say good-bye to Nan and she came out.

"Claude, I'm really sorry," she said. "First times are always tough."

"Forget it."

"Come see us soon," she said. "I mean it."

"I will."

I touched Claude's shoulder, and said goodnight—that's all— and shut the front door. I followed Nan upstairs. We'd left everything dirty behind, not even the table cleared, although she had remembered to blow out the candles.

"Doria's shy. Who wouldn't be with a father they've never met? How can we blame her?" I said to Nan's back when we were almost at the top.

Nan turned to look at me, her face contorted with pain. I stopped where I was.

"That's not the point. Don't you understand why Claude is here, Martin? He came to Cambridge to see his daughter because he thought she would take care of him as he's dying. Don't you understand how sad this whole thing is? You never understood that this is what he was doing, making a home for himself with a family to surround him? And she couldn't care less—she couldn't even stand to spend a whole evening with him. How could you not get it, Martin?"

I stood wordless on the stairs.

"Say something, Martin."

"I don't know what to say, Nan."

She continued up to our bedroom, and I turned around to go down again. I'd understood something, though—I'd been right, intuitive from the beginning, about Claude's wanting, but did I understand that want, see it was fueled by fear? I only understood what I could—that we do our best to account for ourselves and our choices. I couldn't see Claude's need to its logical end, to its grave.

And then tonight—it's been almost two months since Doria was over that one time (Claude sees her for coffee and that's about it, and sometimes she stands him up but he doesn't seem to mind)—I was in the kitchen watching out the window while Claude and my wife were sitting in the wicker chairs I'd put out on the lawn where I was doing some work earlier. I don't know what they were talking about, my hands were full of basil leaves, but their faces glowed. And then they got up and walked over to the bush, my burning bush with the white flowers. Both Nan and Claude held handfuls of flowers, cupped like something delicate and sexy, and then they moved together. With empty hands, his fell on her shoulders, hers on his, and they kissed. There was no head twisting, no penetrating tongues, just pressure, and his hand moved to her left breast, the one closest to me, and stayed there for a few seconds. I could have been either one of them at the moment, I knew how both sides felt. Then it was over, the night was darker, water running over my hands, and can I say that I'm not jealous or even angry? They wouldn't want me to be—anyone (but it is me I'm talking about, my window, my wife) would have watched what was happening, but they'll never know that I felt, and now still feel something else. I'm overcome—it's not a word I like, but here it is—with the heaviest sadness I'll ever know. I don't want to cry—a disease is there, what can I do about it? We do what we can to make each other feel loved and safe.

And now I look up to see my wife in our bedroom upstairs folding clothes into a suitcase. I have good eyes, it's a low window and the suitcase is on the bed, and I've stepped way back here in the full fragrant green of my garden. I see a pair of her pants go in, then her blue sweater, and now a peach-colored satin summer nightgown I bought for her last year, the one she only wears when she feels good about herself. And that folds into the suitcase like thick cream on top of cream, so unbearably soft I almost don't want to watch, but I do. And then a shirt of mine goes on top of her satin thing—she's packing for me, my clothes rough by comparison, crude in their lines and buttons and sharp collars, and again, what is happening is almost too unbearably sweet and soft to watch. I'll pretend I saw nothing of anything.

How quickly it all happened. The story is really very clear, very simple, extraordinarily chronological in its retelling, like real life. Claude came and went.

My son will marry a woman I've never met the day after tomorrow, and that is something else. By now I've drowned this bush—its roots are exposed like skinned tendons—and I won't know until tomorrow—no, probably the day after tomorrow—whether or not this will have really changed my life in any way I'll feel later on.

THE SPIRAL

My wife is coming down to tell me she's going out. She could yell instead and minimize the interruption, but she needs to look at me with that certain tilt of her head, to make some contact, to note where I am. I see her feet in their brown pumps on the stairs, now her ankles, the boniest part of her, now her round calves, and maybe for a split second the flat inside of her left knee, and as she takes the last spiral, I see all of her all of a sudden, and she's standing there, her head 30 degrees to the right to match me, semi-reclining. She's looking at my shoes on the beige arm of the couch.

"Honey," she says, her hands in her coat pockets fiddling with something, a lipstick or a wrapped mint, "wouldn't you like me to get your slippers for you?"

I shift into an even deeper position and cross my ankles. "No thanks, Julia, not necessary, I'm just fine this way," I say.

I know that she's annoyed now and we both know her suggestion was not one to make me more comfortable, but to get my feet off the furniture.

"Okay then," she says, wiping her straight brown bangs off her forehead. She is wearing a lot of makeup, and underneath it she is a beautiful woman of forty, with bones as solid as bronze. "I'm going to have coffee with Warren."

Warren is her editor friend who works at a magazine, the one I call the Journal of Pretension. They met when she published her first article—some style piece, I think it was—with him a few years back, and now she needs her daily fix of the man, her daily infusion of who is doing what where.

"Can I get you something while I'm out, John?" She blots her lips with a tissue.

"Pick up some ginger beer," I say. "A six-pack." I know that this will probably send her out of her way, possibly cutting short her time with Warren—that is, if she chooses to remember at all. "Oh, and say hi to Warren for me."

"Right," she says, blows me something like a kiss, and goes up the spiral staircase. She knows I don't like Warren much.

Julia's head has already disappeared when I see her stocking snag on a leaf of peeling paint on the stair post. It's a perennial problem in our house, not just the peeling, which we've painted over and over—nothing adheres to cold metal, it seems—but the staircase itself.

So I shout up to her, "There's another reason to get rid of the damn thing, Julia. See?"

And there's one more thing about the staircase; if a person, let's say my wife, is going up, her head disappears before her body, and so I was talking to Julia's feet, and I don't know if she even heard me or simply opted to ignore me, and that's not only disconcerting, it's wasteful. These days we fight about getting rid of the staircase, or more precisely, I do, since she'd like it to stay. It's hard for me to use with my leg a little off, it makes it hard for me to get out and to get to her upstairs, but she argues that it would cost too much money to remove and replace, and that the house would never look quite right again. But I sense she has other reasons, and none that make me feel wanted in my own home.

When I hear the front door shut, I reach for my notebook again, which had been open promiscuously across my chest when

Julia came down. It's not that I want her to read what's there, quite the opposite, it's that I know she won't even try. I've been retired for almost a year now from the business of law, senior partner (at times it felt as though I was running the place myself, I'd been there so long, tired but never burned-out). My wife of nine years, twenty-five years younger, seems to think I've retired from everything, that I read thrillers, scribble, and snore away the day. I don't think she wonders about me downstairs while she devotedly works above on her various articles and the necessities of her life, going in and out and making this career of hers happen, while I'm like some homunculus banished to the basement. She must think my needs are minimal and my mind has lost its sharpness.

These stairs, I can take them maybe twice on a good day, but on a bad day, once I'm down, they seem insurmountable, they toss my age in my wrinkled face, and I slink back. I feel like Sisyphus on a helix.

I pick up my pen again and look over what I've written that day, in between a little snooze and a trip to the bathroom and one to the kitchen for some saltines. I'm at the scene now—this is the real thing, no fiction here, real as though I'm there at this moment—where the doctor discusses treatments for my first wife's breast cancer. We sit in his office waiting to hear him offer more options—or more optimistic ones, I mean—when there isn't any more he can give us. He raises his eyebrows, waiting for us to speak next—as though we'd ever know what to say—and I see my wife twist her red linen dress over her knees. I find my eyes tearing as I reread what I've written. Not that I write so well. I still have that professional bluntness, the way things happen, and all the facts, but I find solace in this horrible time again, and I smile because it's more than I've felt in a long while, the suffering of my first wife, mother of my only child, of us as two, and my own solitude right now, and I've been wanting to do this for years. It keeps me dark company down here alone.

Some days, though, I wish Julia would ask me what I was working on, or doing, as she did when we were first married and she thought she might learn something from me, older and more articulate. I know she doesn't avoid it because she's not curious—that's one of her strengths, one of the reasons I loved her in the beginning—but because she knows I probably wouldn't tell her if she asked. And that pretty much sums up the state of things in our marriage and in our home, and on our two separate floors. I don't know how this happened.

Another afternoon, and Julia is out again. She is a tireless peddler of her goods, and she reminds me of myself a while back, when I gathered clients as easily as I now brush crumbs off the breakfast table. I am spilling my guts to the wrong man. He is just an architect, bow-tied and intellectually constrained, and not a shrink, and I should just give him the facts about the staircase—it's iron, it twists in a tight spiral, it separates the first floor (bedroom, Julia's study, bathroom) from the lower floor (kitchen, living room, another bathroom, my study, some storage)—and not a psychobiography of my relationship to the thing.

But I can't help myself. When Julia and I bought the Georgetown condo in 1983, as newlyweds, it was the staircase that sold us really. The place was just a bit too small (my daughter would be going off to college in ten months), but full of oddities and charm that made my second-time-around marriage, and her first, seem like fate. I remember whispering to Julia in our bed, when we were still living in my old apartment and we hadn't made an offer on the condo yet, about the parties we would give. I knew everyone in those days, I lived it up and entertained a lot, and Julia wanted to meet them all. At one time, having spotted me at a party, she'd even wanted to meet me, and so she had, and our joining was efficient and irrefutably flattering.

"People will descend to get to us," I said to her, twisting my finger through the air like one of our guests on the staircase. "It will be an attraction, a novelty, leading to something so intimate and the only place to be. Darling, we'll have parties where no one will ever want to leave."

Julia kicked off the covers, lifted her leg, and pointed her toe. "And I'll be able to show off my legs to their full advantage as I descend with my wit," she laughed.

Yes, those legs were lovely then, and so was her self-confidence. She'd been liberated from years of dissatisfaction and nasty men, fleeing free into the idea that I could give her everything she wanted, that her mind would finally be out of a box with no light, that I was everything to her.

The next morning we made an offer on the condo, and on the day we moved in she descended the spiral staircase nude while I was unpacking some books. Julia was proud of her reference to high art—and how quickly I picked it up, even for a lawyer—and that made us both feel so good about ourselves we made love on the same beige couch we still have, and I was amazed by her young body. And now she worries about my shoes on the upholstery.

"But that was years ago," I say to the architect, the son of a friend, "and we don't do much entertaining these days."

"I understand," he returns the sympathy, and looks at me as though he really would have preferred me to keep all this stuff to myself (his eyes suggest that he is too young to hear about this kind of historical dissolution, when he is still being created).

"You see," I go on, "my study is down here, but after an hour or so in it in the morning, I come out here to the light. I watch the vines whip across the window, or errant garbage litter my property, or the crocuses strain in the dirt—I can also lie down—and this makes me happy, and happy makes me productive. Anyway, the thing's a little hard for me to use now." I pat my leg—a varicosity, like a walnut under my silver skin, removed recently. The surgery was not nearly as painful as the discovery or the slow recovery. "It's hard for me to get upstairs, to be with my wife, you know, to get out."

The architect doesn't ask why Julia doesn't come down then, come to me, but takes some notes instead. "Well, no, but this is good you said something," he says, not looking at me. "I know why you were attracted to the staircase in the first place. Maybe we can retain some of that regional aesthetic charm with a more conventional construct. It may be problematic, but not untenable."

I hurry him up and out before I ask him where he learned to talk like that and make him feel self-conscious and bad (as I often did with my young colleagues, telling myself that they deserved it, they had to be tough and exacting), before Julia returns from her daily dose of outside—the moving world. I could just have the staircase torn out without her permission (I'm the one with the money), but that seems a huge and unforgivable breach of our fidelity, so we'll just go around and around on this for a while, as though our fighting isn't a breach of sorts too, a slower and more destructive one at that, a slow descent into total marital disintegration.

I'm at the part in my story now where I feel my first wife's tumor, like a clove of garlic in her breast. She sucks in her breath and tells me that my fingers are icy, and I cry on her forearm. For weeks, I've been able to write only four or five words an hour, and the staircase has not been so much on my mind, nor has Julia, busy with something long I probably couldn't help her with anyway. I want to be a captive downstairs for now, I don't want to get out, or be bothered at the moment. I just want to work, and work through this part.

But Warren has come over early, as usual—it's this kind of thing that makes me dislike him. Julia is still dressing, and so she sends him to me. As he comes down the stairs, I see that Warren has adopted that particularly affected style of dark slip-on shoes with dark socks, and pants that lap almost to the toes like obscene tongues. I sit up and shut my notebook. I consider slipping it under a cushion, but that seems a little silly.

"John, don't get up," Warren says. I can tell he has just shaved that baby face of his because his skin flashes in different shades of pale. He reminds me of someone in a Victorian novel who dies after breaking a leg trying to catch a lady's hat which has floated away in the breeze. Gallant but a little embarrassing.

"How's it going, Warren? Nice tie you have on."

"Oh this? Thanks," he says, touching the silk. "Sorry you won't be coming with us tonight, John." Warren disappears into the kitchen as though it's his own place, and I hear him pour a bag of Goldfish into a bowl and pop open a Diet Coke. "I was hoping that you'd be able to point out the big names to me."

It doesn't seem to occur to Warren that if I were going to the party, he wouldn't be. Or maybe it does occur to him. Julia never misses a party if she thinks it might be worthwhile, but when I do, she takes Warren, who is infinitely available when my wife calls. Warren looks especially sexless at present (no, he definitely is not putting it to my wife—or anyone, I assume).

"Just not up to it tonight, Warren. I'm sure that you and Julia will do fine without me," I say. "Would you mind getting me a ginger beer?"

Warren looks a little perplexed, as though he's wondering if he's being bossed around. I give him a little nod to show that yes, he is being bossed around just a bit, nothing serious, but whose house is this, whose invitation, whose wife?

"I don't know how you can drink this stuff," he says, bringing me back a bottle but no glass. "It tastes like medicine."

"Love it," I say. And I do love the way it burns my throat as it goes down. We sit silently for a few minutes, crunching away on the crackers. Warren blows the salt off his fingertips. Upstairs, I hear Julia drying her hair.

"Jules, hurry up," Warren shouts up the stairs, and checks his watch afterward. I want to tell him that it is supposed to be the other way around, but I'm so overcome with this assertion that he is absolutely no replacement for me—I mean really, how can he be, but what is he then?—that I don't.

"You'd think you'd have learned by now, Warren, that she's never ready when she says she will be. Just come a half hour later than she tells you to and you'll never have to wait."

"You would think I'd have learned, wouldn't you?" he agrees. "What are you working on there?" He is pointing to the notebook in my lap.

I'm sure he's surprised by the way I snap the book to my chest. "Just scribbling," I say. "Nothing that would interest anyone."

"May I look?" I shake my head. "Julia says you won't show her either, so we've decided you're writing dirty stories."

"That's what you've decided, is it?" I retort. "I don't suppose the Journal of Pretension would be interested in that sort of thing, would it?"

One thing about Warren, he takes teasing well—and he assumes that this is teasing, these put-downs, though sometimes I'm not sure. He once told me I reminded him of his father, a urologist with a cutting sense of humor.

"Julia—we—wonder why you're so secretive about it, that's all," Warren says. "I mean, you are her husband, and even she doesn't know what you are doing."

"Thank you for telling me, Warren." This is news to me, that they've discussed my notebook.

"I'm her friend, John," Warren says, and shrugs. He tries to crush the Coke can with one hand, but the metal bends only slightly under the pressure. He is known to be very good at what he does at work. I imagine he's one of those passive-aggressive types.

Julia winds down the spiral staircase just then in her black mini dress, kicking up her legs and humming.

"Do we have time for a drink first, Warren?" she says.

Warren goes into the kitchen to make her a martini and she stands over me and looks down, so I run my hand up her stockinged leg and feel the callous on my index finger catch on her nylon. Maybe now I'd like her to stay.

"You sure you don't want to come, sweetheart? What are you

going to do for dinner? You could have some Chinese delivered," she says, and strokes the top of my head. Dinner is always when she comes downstairs, it is still the thing we do together.

"Me and the micro." I remove my hand from her leg. "We'll be fine."

"There's a Lean Cuisine in the freezer," Julia says, and extends her hand out for the drink Warren offers her. He gazes at her so adoringly I wonder what he sees when he looks at her. Julia sighs after her first tiny sip. "A little fortification never hurt."

"Promise you won't desert me at this party, will you, Jules?" Warren says and then turns to me. "She knows everyone, you know that? She makes me feel like I just arrived in town."

"You're too modest, and you're a big man, Warren," I say to him. "Eat 'em alive." Which is probably what he does—he'd have to in the business—although it's quite hard to imagine.

Julia gives me an impatient look. "Let's go then," she says, feeling her hair, checking her earrings. "Don't stay up too late, John. You look tired. Sure you're okay?"

"I intend to have several wild parties while you're gone. You don't know what you're missing here, me and my dirty stories."

"Oh, John," Julia sighs again, "sometimes you make me feel so depressed. Can't you just say, 'Have a nice time,' or something like that? It was your decision not to come, your decision to stay balled up down here. Don't make me feel bad for going. Honestly."

"Honestly then, have a nice time," I yell to the two of them as they disappear up the staircase. I'm a bastard, but now I've made it so that I'm glad to be left alone. These interruptions break my thought, and these days Julia just breaks my heart all the time. I blame myself in part, but I have tried to get to her.

Over the phone I order more Chinese food than I'll ever eat, because I have an idea about seeing those white cartons piled in the refrigerator the next morning, and eating out of them with chopsticks while I sip hot coffee and get started on the chapter where we tell our daughter that her mother is going to die. Baby corn, tree ears, Shanghai noodles, French roast, 2 percent milk, maybe six months.

I don't want to have to scramble up the stairs in order to get the door when it rings, so I go up as soon as I'm off the phone. By the time I've made my way up, clutching at the railing, feeling the cold metal on my hand, and really tightening my grip, I am alarmed at the throbbing in my leg and behind my left eye, and I down a couple of Advils in the bathroom. I tell myself I'm not dying just yet, that the pain is from inertia.

It's strange to be alone upstairs, no Julia in bed or getting dressed. It could be a long time before my food arrives, so I sit at her desk and turn on the lamp. Everything is orderly, like she is, and smells of her perfume, and for a while I don't touch anything but lean back in her chair and feel the pillow embroidered with her initials press into the small of my back. When I look up, I see myself looking back at me in the full-length mirror opposite the desk. I could be interesting in this seat, literary even as a stretch, and I wonder if Julia watches herself at work. That would be like her. It's part of the total picture.

I'm suddenly reminded of my mother-in-law's apartment in Boca Raton we've visited a few times, where a full-length mirror faces you as you sit on the toilet. I can't figure out why you'd want to watch yourself going to the bathroom with all those contortions and indelicacies. It's like watching yourself cry, or maybe even make love—some things you shouldn't see. The blur is gone, the moment is lost, the self-consciousness crowds in.

Julia has placed a recently published magazine article of hers about superstitions on top. She never showed it to me or asked for my advice or help in writing it as she used to do, and as I read through it I see that she is really very good and probably doesn't need my help at all. She has surpassed me. I am obsolete, but shouldn't that make me feel fine in a way for what she may have learned from me? Or maybe the sight of her own face—not mine—her own mouth forming the words, staring back at her from the mirror, is all she needs right now.

Under the article there is a yellow pad with a few lines in her tiny script, so delicate, and the heading "article, maybe."

"A good marriage is that in which each appoints the other guardian of his solitude." Rilke, I think. Check? Reader, I married him.

"Oh, Julia, how could you?" I laugh—she still likes those references—and then suddenly I'm crying, so that by the time I go to the door for the Chinese food I startle the deliveryman with my blubbering eyes and wet mouth and don't even bother to make a threatening remark about how long it's taken. Now I'm worried enough about myself to eat all the food while I watch something on television that is mildly interesting and effectively distracting. I fall right into bed and sleep, my fingers still greasy, my lips still sweet, and my stomach round and hard and comforting from too much food.

I hear Julia in the room—I see that it's after midnight—and she's obviously tripped on one of the cartons I left on the floor and is bending down to remove it from her shoe.

"Jesus, what is this?" she hisses in the dark, holding it up.

"Chicken with broccoli and black mushrooms, I think," I murmur from the bed. "Or noodles." The bathroom light outlines my wife from behind and she moves toward me and sits on the bed.

"Thanks. John, you're still dressed. Are you okay?"

"I'm fine," I say, and pull her down to me. I am glad to see her and touch her now, but then she sits up and begins to take off her earrings with efficient pulls. Clip clip.

"I wish that you'd eat downstairs instead of up here. Our bed is not a kitchen." Julia stands to remove her dress, and then goes into the bathroom.

"I'm not a captive down there," I say, over the running water. "That is not my dungeon. Sometimes I come up for you, you know."

"Warren got drunk tonight," Julia informs me when she returns from the bathroom brushing her hair. "He fell in the hall— fortunately no one saw him."

"That Warren," I say. "Is he the greatest, or what?"

"Everyone kept asking me where you were. Some of your former colleagues were there. I think it made Warren feel bad."

"They probably assumed he was your gigolo."

"You're cruel. I wanted you to go with me, I asked you to come."

"Actually, if you remember, the invitation was mine to begin with," I say. I don't know why I am so cruel, really, why I do this at all to her. "I wanted to work. I was fine alone."

Julia slips naked next to me in bed. She smells like perfume and overheated clothes. "Are you sure you're okay?" I nod under her touch, it's what I need at this moment I hate myself. "Well then, you should get up and brush your teeth. Your breath smells like garlic."

"O lovely Pussy, O Pussy, my love, what a beautiful Pussy you are, you are, you are," I sing to her.

"Oh, John, Jesus, go to sleep, please," my wife says to me, and rolls in the other direction.

I know that she is on the edge of sleep when I talk. "Jule, what if I had fallen down the stairs at eight and you didn't come home until after twelve and I was lying down there, bleeding, dead? I don't know how you could leave me for so long, why you don't worry."

I can tell she's figuring out what to say to me, and she rolls onto her back. "But John," she says so sweetly, my name as I first heard her say it, that I can almost imagine we still love each other, "you didn't fall."

She brings me breakfast in bed the next morning. In a pale pink robe, she is lovely.

"I'm sorry," she says, placing the food before me. I am eating upstairs again. I don't want to know what Julia is apologizing for just then, and there are so many ups and downs to this marriage I'm getting dizzy.

How can a daughter take the news that her mother will be dead in six months? Mine, only eight years old, wouldn't take it at all.

Can we go get the doll whose eyes open and shut? she asked. Her mother whispered to me to get in the car right then and go to the toy store, which I did, but I found myself unable to decide between the doll that was dressed in summer cotton and the one in a woolen bunting. It was late October then, and I was as young and blind as a child myself, and so I bought both, sending my wife into the bedroom and my daughter into such a state of confusion, her blue eyes shut tight, and—

"John, Warren's going to be here soon," Julia says from upstairs.

"No, Julia, he can't come now, I'm working," I yell back. Those fucking baby dolls—I don't even know what happened to them. I do remember their eyelashes, sharp as the edge of a scallop shell.

Julia comes down two steps and leans over to look at me. "We go through this every Sunday, do you know that? Warren comes over to play cards with me, and you throw a fit. I swear you look forward to it."

"Julia, I'm working. It's very important now that I do. Play cards upstairs."

"Why don't you go into your study?" she says. "You don't need to work in the living room."

"I need to work where I need to work, dammit." I feel my face bulging with frustration. "And this is where I need to work, Julia. Okay?"

"I don't even know that you are working," she says. "Who the hell knows what you're doing?"

Now I hear her answer the doorbell, and there's something in the tone of her voice that makes me think she is cautioning Warren against me this afternoon, as she should. I am particularly pissy, I have accused myself of everything. Warren's voice rises in question. Julia repeats what she'd already said, and Warren moves to the stairs.

"Hey, John," he yells down, "I picked up a book for you today. You're going to love this."

I see Warren's loafers on the stairs, the flash of some swirling patterned socks, and the stiff cuff of his corduroy pants. "I was at the Lodge Bookstore this morning, just looking around, and there was this book, by a lawyer, no less, about how to write your own autobiography."

He is still at the top of the stairs, stopped as though he's not sure if he should come down, given how Julia has warned him.

"As opposed to someone else's autobiography?" I shout up to him. "And what makes you think I'd be interested in that?"

He is bending down and looking at me through the bars, gauging me in some way.

"I assume that's what you're working on, always holed up down here," he says. "Anyway, that's what Julia and I decided. We dropped the dirty story theory."

Is the notebook burning in my hands? My first wife had lost so much weight by the end that her eyes seemed too heavy in her head, and she closed them, especially when she talked to me. Didn't she want to see me as long as she could?

I look up in time to see Warren's left foot miss the edge of the iron step and his body somehow turn over on itself—weirdly, I'm thinking of fiddleheads—and fall down the staircase in a perfect spiral, sliding almost, headfirst, clickety-clack on the metal with his feet after him, his stiff heels ticking the steps. The book has fallen long before him, open like a split torso on the rug.

And then his head is on the carpeted floor while his right foot still rests on the riser. A fringe of Warren's scarf is tucked into the corner of his mouth, and his eyes are tiny and darting furiously. He's not moving, but I can still hear the clickety-clack. I kneel over him and see a line of blood as thin as a thread on the underside of his chin. It's beginning to stain the collar of his shirt.

Julia is above me and her face looks flat from where I am.

She screams, "Jesus, Warren, are you okay? Warren? Is he okay? Oh, do something."

"Warren," I say softly, "are you all right?"

Warren mumbles something to me, but with Julia still screaming I can't hear him.

"Warren?" I touch his shoulder. His body trembles from shock and I bend a little farther down.

"No," Warren says. "I'm not okay."

I rise on one knee and place my hand up to quiet my wife, trapped upstairs above us and looking down, as Warren is blocking her way.

"Julia, I want you to calm down for a minute," I say. I've never seen her look so young, and why is a woman's hand over her mouth such a feminine gesture? "I want you to let go of the railing, I want you to back up and get to the phone, and then I want you to call 911. And I want you to wait until they come, because I can't exactly come up there to let them in myself, if you see what I mean."

She nods, and is gone. I'm so calm as I wait kneeling next to Warren, so calm as I answer Julia's hysterical questions when she's off the phone, I really wonder if I can feel anything anymore. Finally, it's hard for me to stand. I've been kneeling for such a long time, I'm frozen stiff.

I'm really sort of stuck now, even with no interruptions. The part where my first wife dies is not the end of what I intend to write, I can't just end it there when the loss goes on, but it's the hardest part, of course, and I haven't been able to get through it. Julia has refused to come downstairs since Warren fell two weeks ago, which means I have to come up with her food or we have to go out for it. I now go up and down freely, and she doesn't, afraid to descend for who knows how many reasons. She assures me she'll get over it, she's recovering too.

It seems a little tacky to bring up the issue of the staircase now (the architect called and prodded in the most obtuse way), with Warren still at bed rest and home from the hospital for a week, his neck mending, his breathing self-regulated so he won't sigh too deeply and crack the thing all over again. Julia reports to me on him daily—he'll be okay but probably won't ride horseback or play ice hockey again, if he ever did to begin with. She seems contrite about something, and grateful to me at the same time, but I don't want to know what it's all about at the moment. I have done nothing anyone should be grateful for.

For now, the arrangement works well. When I wanted to get up to Julia, she kept me down below, but now when she needs me I come up when I'm good and ready. And the interruptions have really been cut down significantly, so that if I get over this hump—hardly just a hump when you relive the death of someone who was your solitude, as Julia seems to understand—I'll finish the book, or whatever it is, and maybe tear down the spiral staircase and join Julia again, and she'll join me, if we'll have each other once more.

Late in the summer of 1993, a hurricane with the gentle name of Tess smashed everything I had into a million pieces. From a window in the cement cooling house where I waited out the storm, I watched the wind suck all the water from the pool, lift the thatch roof from the tiki hut, and detonate the last of the beach chairs. Square by square, the dining room patio was untiled, and just before Tess changed course, a single wave plucked out the entire length of dock.

Hours earlier, my staff had left for the main island, cramming themselves into four tiny boats that seemed more dangerous than any hurricane. I'd told them to take what food they wanted from the kitchen freezers—we'd lose power and it would all spoil— but they still hid it in their bags and under straw hats. They yelled that I was a crazy yellow-haired man to stare a hurricane in the eye. "She will think you're making fun of death," they warned, shielding themselves from the hot wind that was already blowing up their bright shirts, "and death will make fun back at you." On this island, superstitions and sightings are as plentiful as the joints of coral that cut your feet in the sand, and so I waved them away.

Weeks later, a few of my staff straggled up the trashed beach looking for work, but the rest had been spooked away for good and I never saw them again. During the next exhausting year, there wasn't a time when I wasn't picking up broken glass or scrubbing away the pocks and pecks of seawater and sand. I hammered shingles onto the roofs of twenty cabanas, quarried slabs of bluebitch stone, rebuilt the dock, spent all the money I had and borrowed more. When the repairs were almost finished, I got on the phone and begged every travel agent I'd ever had anything to do with in my fifteen years as owner of this place (at twenty-five I had taken over from my mother, now retired to the heart of Manhattan), to steer clients my way. They promised they'd do what they could.

Finally, at the height of my first season back in business, from behind the rethatched tiki bar, I stood for a moment and looked gratefully out at my guests around the pool. Five women from a book group ordered drinks from Tom, who was stiff and unsure in his khakis and flowered shirt, when he was used to carrying buckets and hammers and wearing nothing but a pair of running shorts bleached gauzy. I expected the women to start reading— the same book, of course—but they gazed at the water instead, hands under their thighs, trying on the unfamiliar work of relaxation. Three men I'd checked in the night before when they arrived from a day of delayed flights and too many mixed drinks were already asleep on chaises, their tight faces to the sun. The Jensen family reunion—thirteen in all—took up more than their share of space with their gear and noise. Scattered couples, including a pair on their honeymoon, filled out the small but adequate crowd. Down at the beach, an awkward man lumbered onto a jet-ski while his wife stood on the sand and shouted cautions at him.

The day was brilliant, the heat tempered by the trade winds, and for a lifting moment I heard the hymn I'd been waiting for since the day Tess tore through. Every host, every cook, every seducer listens for his particular sound, and mine was the simple noise of my existence—people at leisure. But despite the sound, I also knew I was barely hanging on to the place I loved so much. I'd left myself no margin for another disaster, and this might be the final decisive season for me. The possibility that I could fail so easily and lose all this—my life, the only place I knew and wanted to be—made me dizzy enough to crouch down and rest my forehead against iced bottles of beer at the base of the bar.

At a sudden shift in the air, I stood again. When I looked past the pool, I saw a deathly figure moving among the shadows. He took forever on desiccated, sticklike legs to move through the low seagrape trees, some of which were badly deformed from the storm. When he stepped out, the bright glare of the sun seemed to shock him absolutely still. His thin, gray lips pursed, and his eyes receded in sore, watery sockets. The hymn died instantly as eyes fixed on the man's distended belly, which urged itself against a pink shirt, and ears attuned to his labored wheeze. Men pulled their knees up, a child fussed, its mother tensed, I held my breath, stunned. Very soon, the man's wife hurried out of the shade to lead her husband to a chair; in a neon pink bathing suit, she looked obscene with health next to him.

I had checked her in the evening before—they were Cecelia and Henry Blaze, from just outside Boston. Henry, she'd explained while signing the registration slip with her own gold-capped pen, didn't travel well, they would skip dinner. Under the bougainvillea'd portico, I could just make out his bent shape among the bags Jono was piling into the cart that would buzz them to their cabana. They were staying for three weeks, Cecelia reminded me as she slipped her pen back in her purse, and she hoped the weather would hold. She was in her mid-fifties, and I could see that she'd been pretty once, but over-efficiency and some sadness had taken it out of her. Distracted by noise in the kitchen at that moment, I didn't think about the Blazes again.

Now as Henry Blaze creaked himself onto one of the pool chairs, I anxiously waited for leisure to return poolside, but I saw from the looks on the faces of the other guests that it wasn't going to come back so easily. No one wants to see reality on vacation, and this was an awful lot of reality on such a bright day. If my first thought about Henry Blaze was get him the hell out of here, my second was, is this death making fun back at me? Tess had nearly wiped me out. After everything, I was not going to let a dead man kill me now.

Before dinner that evening, I searched for my one remaining pair of long white pants and linen shirt. My cabana—bedroom, sitting room, bathroom—was the only place that still looked like the hurricane had just blown through. I had replaced the broken windows, but the roof continued to leak and the floor buckled. My bed was unmade—I didn't allow housekeeping in here—the unused half covered with papers, clothes, music tapes I had ordered through the mail, a plate and coffee cup from breakfast.

Some views might be bigger, but I liked the one from my bedroom best. A blue lozenge of water glimmered at the end of a tunnel of seagrape leaves, a less-is-more equation of beauty, and for a seductive second I was stuck on it. I heard calm among the guests, the routine clink of drinks being served on the dining room patio, the two young men I'd hired the week before joking as they put away beach equipment. I had a startling flash of Blaze among the trees, and the possibility that I might lose all this— and then where would I go?—hit me for the second time that day. The outside world seemed tremulous and without borders.

It was too late to iron my shirt once I found it, so I tried to smooth out the wrinkles as I walked to the dining room where the guests were already attempting to outdo each other with descriptions of the sunset. Relieved that Blaze was not around—I assumed he was eating in his cabana and I was spared for the moment—I entered the room as the perfectly confident proprietor.

The book group, shiny in sundresses, ordered a bottle of wine as I stood by their table, hands behind my back. I inhaled their smells that made me a little forgetful as I leaned over glossy shoulders to pour. One of the women had a wonderful, shocked laugh and a head of spiky hair I liked. At another table, the Jensens already had the waiters in a state of mild panic, which seemed to give Bob Jensen a feeling of great power. I'd seen this type before, entitled not by the having of money, but simply by the spending of it. Still, I couldn't deny that the table exuded a kind of welcome, affluent energy.

"How are you all doing?" I said, placing my hand on Jensen's shoulder. I felt the burn on his thick skin through his shirt—I wasn't surprised he'd flipped the sun the finger. He ordered a beer, while some of the older Jensens looked like they'd slipped gently unnoticed into a fugue state. It is true that this business only survives on repeats and referrals, so I brought maraschino cherries for the kids and a very cold beer for Bob Jensen.

I did the room from table to table, made up for the lags the new cook and dining room staff left. This was the head-filling work I was at ease in, the careful organization of a meal, the murmurs of diners, the matte of the red tile floor which would later be mopped down for the night. I heard tones of teasing waft out from the kitchen, and I stared at the spiky-haired woman from the book group, her dress drooping on her shoulders to reveal a glistening chest. I wondered what it would be like if she came back to my wind-whipped cabana and lay on my bed; I'd done this enough times over the years to pacify myself, but never for love. She reminded me that I hadn't stopped to read a book in a long time, and it had been even longer since I'd slept with a woman.

There was a hiss of rubber on the tile just then, and the sound made me recall riding my tricycle around the dining room in the windy off-season, skirting the tables like street corners and stoplights I'd seen in the picture books my mother gave me. But the hissing was Cecelia Blaze, or rather the portable oxygen tank she pulled behind her on a small dolly as she entered the room, clear tubing and the mask draped on a metal hook. She stopped to watch her husband in a white shirt and a pair of beltless pants step cautiously over the threshold of the dining room. The tufts of hair on his alabaster scalp had been combed into temporary compliance.

I showed the Blazes to the last empty table, between the Jensens and the book club. Cecelia ordered for both of them, and when the bisque came, Blaze sipped his loudly and banged the bowl with a large gold pinkie ring set with a red stone. Cecelia did not look at her husband, but stared at the view as she ate. I wondered what twist had led her to marry this older man—and what crueler twist had led them to plague me now.

Blaze didn't look up when I stood by their table, and I could tell he was accustomed to not responding until he was good and ready, that he'd once been in charge of people and things. Cecelia and I talked about hikes she might take, and when I asked if she were interested in a jet-ski—I was only trying to feel something out about these people, what would stir or startle them—she laughed, grateful, I think, for even this lame bit of flattery.

"How about me?" Blaze said.

It was more than I'd heard him say before, and the strength of his voice was unsettling, when I had expected something closer to a rasp or a whisper. His wife pretended he hadn't spoken at all and went back to her soup.

The book club ordered another bottle of wine, and when Blaze began to wheeze, I hurried to pull the cork and pour, to catch the eye of the spiky-haired woman, to make conversation and offer distraction. Cecelia slowly touched her mouth with a napkin and put it by her plate before she stood. A sense of urgency had gripped me and the room, which was now watching the scene with distaste. She began to fumble with the tubing from the oxygen tank, and small words tumbled from her lips. Blaze's shoulders heaved in an increasingly labored way. A waiter stopped short with his tray of melting ice cream for the Jensens.

"Here, let me help you," I offered, and bent down next to Cecelia, who was now kneeling, her skin pale against the red tiles. Her skirt was unwrapped up the length of a freckled thigh, revealing sad white underpants.

"I have it," she said, but continued to pull uselessly at the tubing.

A nervous odor rose off Blaze. I was now almost cheek to cheek with his wife, and a little desperate. "The goddamn thing's taped up," I said.

Cecelia shot me a look of disapproval. She flipped her skirt shut, sat back, and with what seemed like total, prideful indifference, tossed the problem to me; her husband was going to die in *my* dining room. Blaze shifted to the right then, and with a small, almost dainty cough, threw up his dinner. A moment later he took a full, wheezeless sigh while a splatter slid off his square knees onto the floor.

I stood too fast and motioned for my staff to come clean up; suddenly they were blind to me, and I was dizzy.

"Goddamn it!" Blaze said. For the first time we looked directly at each other, and I saw from his eyes that he wasn't really old at all. I could have felt sorry for him then—all this misery in a man just sixty—but I was even less forgiving than earlier that he'd chosen my place for this freak show of his.

After some cleaning up, Cecelia slouched her husband out of the room. I assured the book group that Blaze would be fine, though I could see them rallying as concerned women now and not vacationers. I sent Jensen another beer, which he received with a shrug, and I turned on the ceiling fan to blow the death smell of Henry Blaze out to sea.

Later, the book club played poker and scattered plastic chips on the patio floor, their tone a little off, like people having a good time at a wake. I heard the clatter of bikes and mopeds behind the kitchen as the staff heckled their way home. In the front office, I checked the computer as I did every night now, to see if new reservations had come in since I'd last looked. There was only one, and that not yet confirmed. I put my head in my hands.

"Jesus H., that was some scene with the old man tonight," Bob Jensen said, peering into the office and startling me. "Disturbing you?"

"Disturbing me? No, just shutting up for the night," I said. I wanted to tell him not to stroll where he wasn't welcome, and I knew by the way he was hanging around that I'd have to open the bar and give the guy a drink on the house pretty soon. I turned out the office light.

"So, I thought he was going to die right there," Jensen continued, as we walked outside. He shivered for a second in the heat. "You know that noise he made, like a spoon went down his garbage disposal. Kind of freaked my wife and kids. Let's not even talk about the spewing."

"Let me get you a drink, Mr. Jensen," I said, and led him to the dark tiki bar. He hoisted himself onto a stool and told me what a nice place I had. With his broad back half turned to me, he watched the anoles skitter by the pool lights and sipped his Cuba Libre.

"Okay, what I'm wondering," he said, "is maybe the old guy could eat earlier or later or in his cabana, or something. You don't think I'm being hard, do you?" Jensen said, his voice falsely sappy. "And I'm not saying he shouldn't be here at all because hey, that's his right too. I just think he could be less here, if you see what I mean. I'm sure I speak for the other guests, and I *know* I speak for the Jensens, all fourteen of us."

"Thirteen," I corrected.

"There's a set of twins," he said, and his tongue explored the inside of his cheek as though now daring me to charge him for one more person, when I'd sat him next to death at dinner. "The ten-year-olds. You probably missed them, everyone always does. Anyway, I'd like to see what you can do about the problem. This is our one vacation a year, know what I mean? We plan to make it a regular thing too, come back here maybe, if all goes well."

The fat fuck was threatening me. "Can I top you off?" I said, holding up the bottle of rum. But he waved it away, finished the rest of his drink in a final gulp, and said goodnight. I saw him jump back as a tiny emerald lizard crossed his path.

The book club quit around midnight and made their way, loopy with booze and solidarity, through the trees. Finally, I could go to my cabana. This not-going-to-bed-before-the-last-guest was one of my mother's more tenacious policies. She'd also say Blaze should stay, and bring him his meals herself if that's what needed to be done to keep him happy and hidden. It was a win-win situation financially, she'd declare—her own uneasiness inconsequential—her eye always on business and the next season. But I simply wanted Blaze gone, off my island before he ruined it. His ghostliness, his precarious hold on things, felt too much like mine at the moment.

Though it was late and I was exhausted, I walked toward the Blazes' cabana. From the path, I could see the two defiant fist-shaped rock outcroppings that towered over an eddying, unpredictable pool below, shaded violet even in the dark. I know my part of the island is inspired with natural, moody beauty, and that night I noticed how a winking luminescence seemed to rise from the coral reefs. Cecelia was playing cards on the open terrace and listening to a symphony on the only radio station we got on the windward side of the island. Henry, in a white robe, was asleep in the hammock chair, his head lolled to one side. Cecelia looked up suddenly, though I don't think she saw me hidden by the curve of the path. She looked pained, as if she'd lost something. She might have simply caught a flash off the water just then that made her want to go home as desperately as I wanted them to leave. For this, for her, I decided to let them have the night.

It wasn't until I was in the light of the bathroom back in my cabana that I noticed the spattering of spew—as Jensen had put it so eloquently—on the cuffs of my pants. I had to scrub with an old toothbrush and a cracked bar of soap to get them clean.

"You want us to leave," Blaze said the next morning when I showed up on the terrace of his cabana. Alone and in the full sun, he sat in the hammock swing again, an open book on his lap. He seemed transfixed by something out on the water.

I hadn't expected to arrive at the point so quickly, and it took me a moment to catch up. "I'm concerned about you, that's all," I said. "We have no medical facilities here that I'd trust to treat anything more than a moped burn or diarrhea. We're really not equipped to handle an emergency."

"Like death, for instance, which is hardly an emergency, Mr. Thierry. I take it your guests didn't like my performance at dinner," he said. "But now Cecelia has those nice bookish women to talk to because of me. They've adopted her, I think."

"Please, Mr. Blaze." My impatience surprised him only a little—I could tell he enjoyed revving people up and letting them whirl uselessly. "I'm trying to hold onto this place, and I do know I can't afford to have guests pull out now because they're unhappy or decide to go somewhere else next year for whatever reason. I'm not sure this is the best place for you to be."

"You mean I'm not an asset." Blaze countered my ugly lack of sympathy and squinted at the water again. "Your guests are too uptight."

"You have to understand my position." The truth was I could only ask him to leave; I couldn't actually force him out.

"I understand your position well enough, Mr. Thierry. Now look at mine."

Blaze was not wearing a shirt, and I saw how trim and beautiful his body must have been before he got sick, before he became distended, toxic and puffy in some places, deflated in others. A bracelet of thin black leather circled his wrist, a strange touch on such a pale American. I was repulsed by his body, and when I turned away I saw what he'd been looking at so intently while we talked. On the large sandbar not far offshore, the honeymooners from Philadelphia were bare-chested, their faces pressed tightly together. She was lying on top of him, while his hands circled the sides of her breasts and then the rise of her ass. Their bright orange kayaks sat nose-first on the sand, the single palm tree fanning a wasted shade over them.

"Not exactly private, is it?" Blaze laughed, a little wistfully, I thought.

I sat down on the low wall. My eyes adjusted to the darkness of the room behind Blaze, and to the squadrons of pill bottles and inhalers on the wicker bureau. Last night's oxygen dolly stood by the unmade bed. For the first time, it occurred to me that Blaze might have AIDS, with his collection of mismatched and terrible ravages. Our island is an oil well of pleasure, and I'd seen enough sick people standing in cool and furtive doorways in town to know this particular disease.

"Why did you come here?" I asked.

"You think I singled you out."

"Seems that way," I said. "There are a million islands, Mr. Blaze. You could have gone to Club Med even—they would have given you your own bikinied nurses round the clock."

"Not my thing, Mr. Thierry." Blaze looked up at the sky. "I can see the hurricane did a lot of damage here. This was the most beautiful spot on earth, and I've been to some pretty spectacular places all over the world. I remember you. I remember your mother too."

"You've been here before?" I asked, skeptically.

"Several times actually, last with my first wife, years and years ago. You must have been around thirteen then, miserable and pimply, performing an impressive repertoire of antisocial activities for the guests. You once stood on a rock and peed into the water while we were having dinner in the dining room. Your mother tried to distract us with shrimp cocktail. Jumbo shrimp, she kept saying, look at the size of their tails. All I saw was your skinny ass in the sunset. Still, I always thought it must have been paradise for you, growing up on this island. And now look at you—all business and good interpersonal skills to boot."

There were times I forgot how much I once hated this place, how I couldn't wait to get away. Despairingly fatherless, I had searched among each season's new arrivals for possible candidates. My mother gave me nothing to go on, though. She claimed to know little about who he was. Not because he'd knocked her up and disappeared, or was some married mystery, I was meant to understand, but because that's how she'd wanted it. Mother and child only, the picture of paradise. I was fathered by some resort guest who'd been turned on by my mother's independence and sharp business sense; her long toes, tanned face, and light eyes; the skittery sounds at night; this place so far from his home; the erotic heat in the dark. All she might have had of him was a credit card receipt in her files.

"Why did you come back?" I asked.

"I heard you were hurting for business, I thought I'd help you out a little."

"But I don't think that's what you're doing," I said. "You are definitely not good for business."

"I want to die here, Mr. Thierry," Blaze said, sounding as tired as he looked all of a sudden. "I was hoping you might be sympathetic."

Removed and up in his windy cabana on the bluff, Blaze stayed away from the other guests, and I had Tom bring him his meals. With Blaze out of my sight, I even allowed myself to feel hopeful and hear the hymn bounce off the bluebitch stone and pool's surface again. The Jensen kids napped by the pool. A man, still laughing, had to be brought back off the water when the breeze died on his windsurfer. The honeymooners slept past lunch; other guests settled into their own muted routines, while I willingly busied myself with work, the supplying of other peoples' pleasure. Cecelia Blaze had been encircled by the book group—they seemed a useful novelty to each other—and her appearance each morning was good news to me and a reminder that three weeks would go by quickly. Blaze would leave, sick but alive, as he had come.

So perhaps it was some blind gratitude finally, or simply curiosity during a hopeful moment, that inspired me to deliver Blaze's lunch myself one noon. Motionless and drained in the shadows indoors, he did not seem surprised to see me, though it had been days. He tentatively examined the tray with his head drawn back, as though the fish might jump up and bite him. I understood then that for someone as sick and weak as he was, the wrong food, wind, breath, dose could easily kill him.

He'd eaten some bad meat in Poona once and had nearly died from it. "My stomach ulcerated. I shit blood," he explained. He took a bite of fruit—he was not starving himself—which he chewed with his front teeth. "You don't know where Poona is, do you, Kip?"

"I haven't done a whole lot of traveling," I said. "Look, I wanted to let you know I appreciate . . ."

"Northern India. That's your geography lesson for today," Blaze interrupted. Did I know he was the largest importer of Indian movies to the United States? The demand was voracious, he explained, not to be believed, and then he pushed away his plate and could barely keep his eyes open long enough to see me leave. When I delivered his dinner, he was in the same place I'd left him earlier, though this time he didn't talk. His lips were chalky from something Cecelia had administered to him, and the air had a cool, ventilated feel to it.

The next day he was a little more alert, and in painfully slow sentences described for me the time he'd spent in the backs of tiny Indian import shops in Queens, Detroit, and Los Angeles, sitting on overturned milk crates with his Indian friends, drinking yogurt shakes and nibbling sweetened fennel seeds. He was hazy with fatigue, full of admiration for the exotic, lost in memory. I felt myself being drawn back to these places with Blaze—I had never known the kind of easy friendship he was describing—but still I was anxious to leave his dark sickroom with its sour, clinical odors.

In spite of my aversion, I fell into a routine of bringing Blaze his meals, perhaps to ensure that he'd continue to stay away from the other guests by satisfying his increasing need to talk. One morning at the end of his first week on my island, I found Blaze in bed, his skin a new shade of green. He'd been thinking of some of the many trips to India he'd made alone, he said, as though I'd always been standing there listening. I should imagine him, he urged, sweating with pleasure in a New Delhi hotel, burning his throat on spices in Madurai, lapping at the hot air with his tongue as he hung out a train window. His large house outside of Boston was full of bolts of silk and painted boxes he had brought back from his trips. The closets stank of vegetal sizing and the oil of polished copper. Cecelia and his two grown daughters had no interest in any of it.

"Can you picture it?" he asked. "Tell me, can you see it?"

I was born on this island, delivered by the cook's grandmother. A lime tree was planted over my placenta. As a child, I'd given names to crabs in the kitchen so they wouldn't be forgotten at dinnertime, I'd followed anoles around trees because I'd been told they led to diamonds. I knew the female pungency of every leaf and the taste of dirt and sun here, but nowhere else.

"Sure," I said, trying appease his growing agitation. "I can picture it."

Blaze was energetically angry all of a sudden, frustrated that he could not describe anything to me with true accuracy anymore: touch, smell, a spinning head, what it felt like to be completely lost. He recalled words these days, he said, only from the practice of having spoken them before. Imagine, he begged, being robbed of everything in the dank of a park underpass in Bombay by a smooth, beautiful Indian boy only moments after sharing pleasure with him. And imagine walking back to the hotel with pockets flapping empty, ribs aching from fear and a few swift kicks, spent and feeling exhilarated beyond belief, as though it was one of the great moments of life.

"I need you to understand," Blaze said.

I understood; he was talking about love. But what did I know about that, or what love would make a person do? "I have to go," I said, and turned away.

There was noise in the bathroom just then that startled us both, the dull thump of Cecelia's wet towel dropped on the floor. Blaze's eyelids fluttered at this sudden reminder of his wife. I sat down on the side of his bed. I wondered then if it was disease itself or the shame of this disease—it was AIDS, I was sure now—that kept submerging so many of his memories, a struggle either way.

Blaze lifted his head from the pillow, moved his hand toward my wrist, and then withdrew. "Do you see why I want to die now?" he said.

Cecelia came out of the bathroom, her fingers inept at the buttons on her shirt, her face pale from what she'd obviously just heard him say. She sat in one of the wicker chairs and crossed her legs.

"Don't be such a priss," Blaze said to her, having regained full breath now. He was unkind; she was long-suffering. They seemed to accept their complicity in the situation.

"He was telling me about some of his trips," I said.

"I'm sure he was." She nodded. "Did he tell you how he once forgot to walk clockwise around a Buddhist shrine?" She began to laugh, and pulled her knees up girlishly. "They nearly arrested him. Oh, I don't know, it just seems like the strangest thing to me."

"Cece," Blaze said, as though he'd been trying to get her to understand forever, "it is so much more than that."

Her face suddenly tightened as she considered him. Was she picturing at that moment her husband bent over another man, thrusting with passion? Was she wondering where his tongue and mouth had been? He must have also slept years of nights in bed with her, the comforter over them with reassuring weight, the dry kiss on the lips as equally reassuring. My husband is not queer, she would tell herself, he does not have sex with men because he is my husband. She wasn't going to indulge or spare him now— his dying was killing her too, after all. She fiddled with her hair while her eyes watered; the love of her life was retreating, and he didn't want her to come along.

That evening, still distracted from the morning's scene with the Blazes, I wandered out onto the patio. The book group, having splintered during their week, was back together for a last dinner, looking forced and tired. The spiky-haired woman touched my hand as I walked by—too little, too late, too difficult, I thought—but she only wanted me to see something.

"Look," she said, and nodded toward the sandbar where Blaze and I had seen the half-naked honeymooners days earlier. I offered a Deserted Evening package—wine and lobster at sunset on the tiny island—for an extra fee. It had been my mother's idea early on, an appreciation of the romantic streak in others. At most, there had only been a few takers a season. "God, it's wonderful to see them out together," she sighed.

At the edge of the sandbar, one of the beach boys was helping Cecelia step out of the dingy. In the evening light, her turquoise dress was diaphanous and slinked around her ankles. Blaze was hunched and uncertain as he lifted his knobby leg to climb out of the boat, one hand heavy on the boy's shoulder. He had not been farther than the terrace of his own cabana in almost a week, and this vastness must have startled him.

Cecelia smoothed a blanket on the sand as the boy left in the boat and Blaze sat down next to her. What a joke to offer up this sandbar as deserted. When you were on it, it felt alone and tiny and the single palm seemed enormous, but from the height of the patio—and from Blaze's terrace, as I had seen—it was a theater stage on which to act out this peculiar marriage. Cecelia's adjustment of her dress, Blaze's shift to one side as he removed something sharp from under himself, the splash as she clumsily poured wine—these were larger than life, lit up for all to see. Blaze had to know this.

We saw how Cecelia wanted to kiss her husband, so when he offered only a cheek, she forcefully took his face in her hands and pulled him toward her, pressing her mouth against his. No one spoke, and Jensen, with his knee bouncing at top speed, stared alternately at his own wife with her broad, peeling nose and at the Blazes. When I smelled the sizzle of garlic, shrimp, and lime juice, I hustled people in, tripping a little over my own feet.

Alone as I watched again in the almost dark, I saw Cecelia drop the dress off her shoulders to reveal her breasts. She straddled her husband, who was on his back, leaned down so her face was against his. They stayed like this for a long time, past the time I heard dinner brought to the tables and the sunset faded.

"You think they're okay?" Jensen said. He had left his family still eating, and stood next to me on the patio. He smelled of steak and pepper. Jensen had continued to poke his head into my office from time to time, giving me a moronic thumbs-up and looking for something to throw his weight against. I knew he was inflated with a dangerous amount of sun and restlessness.

"I'm sure they're fine," I told him, but I wasn't sure at all, and was immobilized by the idea that Blaze was finally dead and Cecelia, in some love/grief clutch, was frozen too. A freak high tide should suck the corpse out to sea and dump it on some other island.

"Let me help you get them," Jensen offered, nodding toward the sandbar. As we went down to the beach and pulled the dingy out, I wondered if I'd misjudged the guy all along—a man who is idle is sometimes not himself, or too much himself. Jensen easily rowed to the sandbar while I was transfixed by the napkin which bloomed from his pants pockets at each stroke.

"Jesus, her dress," Jensen said to me. "Hey there," he yelled to Cecelia. "Everything okay?" We were eddying in the water, Jensen's oars firm against the night's stronger and deeper current.

Cecelia slid off her husband ungracefully and covered herself as she rose from all fours. "I didn't want to wake him up. I guess I didn't realize how late it is."

"Time to come back." I jumped out of the boat and dragged it up to the sandbar with Jensen still sitting in it, sucking his teeth and showing no intention of getting out.

Cecelia leaned down toward her husband. When he opened his eyes, I could tell how disoriented he was by the water at eye level, the dark.

"I can't move," he said.

"Oh, come on, Henry." Cecelia put her hands on her hips.

"It's late. These men are waiting. Try." She touched his leg with her foot.

"What's up?" Jensen yelled from the boat.

"I'm all gripped up, Cece," Blaze said. "I'm sorry."

Cecelia turned so closely to me I thought she was going to collapse against my chest, but it was only so she could whisper. "This happens sometimes when he's still for a long time, so you're going to have to carry him." Then she stepped back and waited, her arms across her chest with that odd indifference again.

I knelt down and lifted Blaze's head off the sand. It was the first time I'd touched him, and I was surprised by his softness. I struggled ineffectively until I called to Jensen. His eyebrows rose as though I'd interrupted him, and then he gestured for me to come close.

"Well, shit, what's wrong with him first, Thierry?" he said. "Cancer, AIDS, something catching? What, before I get my hands all over him."

I hesitated for a second and looked at his unpleasantly red face. "I don't know, Mr. Jensen. I'm not a fucking doctor."

I stared at Jensen with obvious contempt while he considered whether or not to hit me. Finally he jumped out of the boat, brushing his shoulder against mine.

"Can you sit?" he yelled at Blaze, as though he were deaf.

Blaze narrowed his eyes even further. "What do you think?"

Jensen and I managed to haul Blaze into the dinghy and lean him against his wife. A small crowd had gathered on the beach, and then, as we were lifting him from the boat, Blaze slipped away from us like a hooked but determined fish. Cecelia and the others gasped, while I wanted to throw my head back and howl with laughter, fall to my knees while the tears streamed down my cheeks. My hands went weak, my bowels and stomach quivered, and Blaze sank fast and helpless in the shallows. It was where he wanted to be, after all. I should just let him go.

But I grabbed him instead. Jensen was stunned and Blaze was

an even more impossible weight now. His eyes were closed, as though he had decided to pass calmly through this humiliation and his failure. Someone had wheeled one of the wooden beach chairs down to the water's edge, and we managed to lay Blaze on it. His dripping clothes hung on the distorted angles of his body, making him look even worse than before. Jensen left, calling to his kids who were gawking over the patio railing as though he hadn't seen them in weeks. People flirted around us for a few seconds, while Cecelia sat on the end of the chair and stared out.

"I need to stay here for a minute," Blaze announced.

"I'm going to get you a blanket, a sweater, something," Cecelia said numbly. She stood and walked away.

"She's weaving—it's the wine." Blaze watched her go, and then pulled a pack of still-dry cigarettes from his shirt pocket. "Have a lighter, Thierry?"

"Jesus Christ," I said, and lit his cigarette. "You're smoking."

"Yes." He took a defiantly deep inhale, and looked pleased with himself. "Live life king-sized."

"What's that supposed to mean?"

"Something I liked in an Indian movie, *The Eighth Moon*. Seen it? A real blockbuster," he said. "Everything's about smoking in that country. The prince has just routed a coup, killed a few hundred ingrates, and so he pulls out a cigarette and lights up. 'Live life king-sized,' he declares. It sounded right."

I sat on the end of the chair where Cecelia had been. Blaze's ankle tapped at my thigh as he dragged on his cigarette.

"This outing tonight was my idea," he said, "so don't blame Cecelia. People say she's too stiff, but that's not really true. I think I didn't give her enough time when I was living—not dying, that is—but I love her. Your little island"—he waved his cigarette toward the sandbar—"seemed like it might be the right way to show her." Blaze laughed and pulled himself higher on the chair. "I have no energy to explain anything anymore, Thierry, my disease, my life, my unnatural passions, as it were. I want to die. Seems I'm not having much luck, though."

"It's a little hard to drown yourself in less than a foot of water." I turned around to look at him. "*You* live life king-sized, Blaze. My business is going under."

"Don't be such a pessimist. It shows a great lack of imagination."

"So what if I lose this place," I said, ignoring him. "I can go somewhere else."

"You don't want to do that. You'd get squashed, Thierry. You're an island boy with your ponytail and skinny legs. Your sneakers are all wrong too. What do you know about anything or anyone? Look, when was the last time you even watched television? Stay, reposition yourself, that's all—change with the times. Maybe you can call this Euthanasia Island, the getaway of a lifetime. Hospice Hideaway. Offer sunset pillow smotherings, poolside morphine drips, the feeding tube extraction. Quick turnover. You haven't been in the real world, Kip—you have no idea how popular this dying thing is." Blaze tossed his cigarette into the water. "I could make it worth your while. Repeats and referrals, the blood of the business. I know everyone, I'd bring them to you, all my friends I've told you about. You help me on my way, and I'll save your business in return."

"You're asking me to kill you," I said.

Blaze tapped his foot against my thigh again. His offer was horribly simple—if I believed him at all. I thought about how many times, after Tess tore through and I was on my knees picking up the endless pieces, I said I'd do anything to save my island. I heard water slide into the sand, heat spiral in the air, the coral reef shift and settle. All my life this sound had been my idea of a perfect night, and always would be, no matter where I ended up.

"I won't kill you, Blaze," I said absolutely. "Not even to save all this." Finally, I was more sure of this than anything else in my life.

"Euthanize is the word, Thierry. It's an act of mercy, not business." He sighed, defeated. "I've been trying to tell you that, to show you. I've told you all my stories now."

Their week over, the book club and other guests left the next day, and I was hardly surprised when Jensen checked out with them, a week early, bullying my office to accommodate his immediate change in plans, dragging his dopey family with him.

The time before a new group of guests arrived had always been a good break for me and my staff, and now I fell into it, grateful for the distraction. The staff talked in full island voices again. Together we ogled over the stuff people forgot under beds and in full view. We ate lunch in the kitchen and sloppy salad with our hands, whisked our bare feet across the floor. Staffers' children, now bravely out from among the trees, wandered around and bounced on the empty beds. I had Tom bring Blaze his meals again, so I wouldn't have to see him. On two evenings, I saw Henry and Cecelia standing on the dirt road that led to the center of the island. I didn't know where they had been or were headed as they looked up at the canopy of trees that kept the moon from lighting their way.

By the middle of the Blazes' second week, there were several last-minute cancellations and occupancy was at an all-time low. I must have seemed shell-shocked as I wandered around, and I felt I'd slipped into some kind of mindlessness. I wondered if this was how Blaze felt, giddy, knowing what would come next, a true dead end, for it was now pretty clear it was over for me. The few remaining guests began to assume the natural liberties that come with an enormous amount of space. Their irritations became public as they echoed off the bluebitch, and they were careless with their things, which I sometimes saw float away with the tide.

One morning I wandered aimlessly behind the kitchen. Inside, a tape played loudly, and I'd been drawn to the open door by the music to watch the women bent and swaying over counters, sweat on the backs of their thick necks, feet slipped out of shoes. I had known them forever, and so I was still paying them with what little I had left, but there was almost no work to do; they were playing cards, sucking on toothpicks, talking. As I watched, I remembered how once one of the staff had come trembling to me. She swore she'd just seen her long-dead father leaning against the kitchen's back door, smoking and waiting for her to get off work, and she wanted me to shoo him away, which I pretended to do. Now I felt those eyes and a hot breath in the shade and left quickly.

That evening, Tom told me the Blazes were waiting for me on the patio. Cecelia was wearing an alarmingly bright dress, huge yellow daisies with blue centers, an ugly island design my mother used to wear on Saturday nights. Henry, in a chair next to her, wasn't eating that day, she told me. First fasting, then a sunset and an enema before bed.

"Like scrubbing the ring off a bathtub," Blaze said. He looked sicker, but also strangely expectant for someone who couldn't expect much of anything anymore. "Has to be done every once in a while so the water's clean. Give it to him, Cece."

"What's this?" I asked, and took the piece of paper Cecelia held out to me. There were fifteen names on the list, all Indian from what I could tell.

"I've invited my friends, just like I told you I would," Blaze said. "You got a few empty rooms at the moment, am I right?"

"A few," I said, weakly. I needed to sit down but leaned heavily against the patio railing, my back to the water.

"Some of them won't be able to come on such short notice, of course," Cecelia said, energized by her sudden usefulness to her husband, even in this deranged task. I couldn't bring myself to look at her, to see what she might or might not understand. "They're Henry's friends, really. You know he was up late last night trying to arrange this over the phone."

"Not easy," Blaze said. "But believe me, I've arranged much more complicated deals than this one. It didn't take much convincing; I offered something for nothing. Most people are pigs."

Cecelia laughed at this, and looked a little surprised at her gaiety. Blaze gave her a puzzled look.

"All these people are coming here," I said to Blaze. "Do I have that right?"

"You didn't think I was serious, did you. I can see it in your face," he said. "But a deal is a deal."

Cecelia ignored her husband, as I'd seen her do so many times before. "He's decided he wants them to be here when he dies. They love him." She slapped her hand over her mouth. The way the lowering sun caught in her eyes, I didn't know if she was horrified, thrilled, or both.

Blaze delivered on his promise, and over the next few days fourteen of his friends came to my island. Each arrival was another weight for me, more evidence of a debt I was expected to pay back. As a group, though, these people brought with them an attractive, buoyant life I'd never seen before, a new hymn that I sometimes found myself swaying to. They enthusiastically loved the place and wandered noisily into the dining room at the last minute and stayed for hours, swam at night, slept most of the morning, talked endlessly to me about the island, the birds, and Blaze.

Sanjiv Bhargava, a large and slickly confident man, was Blaze's closest friend among the group, and often sought me out with earnest questions of natural history and my childhood on the island. Three of the guests brought wives who rubbed oil on their dark skin for hours and melted into each other around the pool. Cecelia looked uncomfortable around them at first, so stiff with her mouth mimicking the curve of her arching hairline. She startled at their hands resting on her arms, her knees, the way they included her.

Blaze sat king-like in the middle, but shut out the sudden activity that now swirled around him. Watching him from the window in the main house that overlooked the pool, I was the only one who noticed that he was in deeper trouble now, that his face contorted with spasms, and he fell asleep with his mouth open. In the space of only a few days, his chest had collapsed so that a hollow preceded him, sat on his lap, sucked up his words. These friends of his—fully paid-for and loving their mid-winter luck—swam and teased, but they never turned their heads to check on him, as though he should be my responsibility now.

One morning Blaze's friends had left him while they went down to the beach. Squinting uncomfortably, Blaze sat in the direct early heat but appeared not to have the strength to move himself. Finally, when I could no longer stand to see him purpling and swelling in the sun, I came out of the main house and moved his chair into the shade. I was quick to hurry away.

"No, don't go yet," Blaze said, and caught my arm. "Tell me, Thierry, how does my future look these days?" The strength of his voice still surprised me.

"I don't know about your future," I stalled. I saw Cecelia and Blaze's friends circling around a pair of sailboats on the beach, considering their next activity. "What do your doctors say?"

Blaze laughed. "You want to know about my doctors? All right," he said. "They are institutionally optimistic. They should all be forced to wear buttons that say, 'Be hopeful,' and at night they should have to lay the buttons down next to their alarm clocks so it will be the first thing they see when they wake up, even before they take a leak. But enough already with the optimism, don't you think? It doesn't do me any good." He nodded toward the beach, his wife and friends, and his eyes teared. "Anyway, I've arranged everything. My friends will be back next year with their big brown families and business partners and silent, glaring grandmas who don't speak English—all on my nickel. So you'll be okay, Thierry, don't worry. Now put me back in the sun."

My mother called a little later. Cold as hell in New York, she said hoarsely, as though clots of snow were lodged in her throat. She'd just walked back from the museum and was thinking of buying a pair of snow pants like the ones all the kids had. Since my mother had left this island—ambivalent, but more than ready—she gorged herself on choice.

"I hear you're running a leper colony down there, you've got people throwing up in the dining room," she said. Her friend at Columbus Travel (sister of the reservationist who'd booked the Jensen family) had called to report. Several others had apparently done the same.

"Yes, a leper colony. We got body parts all over the place, but we can fit fifteen people in one bed." I wondered what she would make of Blaze, still alone and in the sun, if she would recognize him through his disease as someone from another time in her life.

"You can joke if you want," my mother said. "But if *I've* heard it, imagine how many other people have too. Word of mouth can kill your business in a second, Kip. I'm absolutely serious, it doesn't take much."

"I know."

My mother sighed. "This man, Jensen, claims he's going to report you—to whom and for what, who knows, but he's telling everyone. At the very least, he's looking for a full refund. There's an asshole in every crowd, remember that—you have to give him the Asshole Special, even if that means crawling to do it to save the business." My mother stopped short. Giving me advice made her uncomfortable when she'd never gotten or asked for any herself. I knew she'd moved over to the window and was thinking, with enormous, familiar regret, how slowly the traffic below her was moving. "Are you in trouble, Kip?"

From my window, I saw one of Tom's young nephews creep past Blaze's chair and slip into the pool. My staff and their kids hissed at him excitedly to get out of the pool which was off-limits, but he dunked and came up sputtering, his eyes completely round as he rubbed his hands across his nipples, electrifying himself. Blaze stirred in his chair and smiled. Some muted chaos had taken over.

"I am," I told my mother just before we hung up.

Blaze threw something into the pool then, a shell he'd had in his curled hand as though he'd been waiting for this, and the children dove for it. The commotion and splashes which landed on his hot face pleased him, but his body seized with pain in retaliation. I thought he might die then, he was so close even if he lived for weeks or months. Would it be so bad to simply help along the inevitable now? I wondered for the briefest moment how it might happen. I could slip him an overdose in a glass of papaya juice which he would eagerly accept. In the privacy of his cabana, I could cover his face with a damp towel and look away. But I'd heard the body struggled violently on its own at the end—a thought that made me sick to my stomach—and who was I to hold this man down?

As I drove Sanjiv into town one morning he told me that he owned a chain of twelve shoe stores in New Jersey and had at least one relative working in every shop. Earlier, he had asked if he could use the kitchen that night—a meal for Henry was what he had in mind—and if I'd show him where he could buy some of the ingredients he needed.

"Full compliance with your requirements and schedule," he had said formally, meaning this was to take place after the regular dinner for the few other guests, and that he would pay for everything. He'd toured the kitchen, walking regally among the staff with their tilted stares and white aprons, found it missing what he needed, hiked up his perfectly pressed black linen shorts, and had given me a broad smile.

I parked the car off the main street, pointed out a few places he might try—though the town was a tourist rip-off and I didn't think he'd have much luck—and told him I'd meet him in the bar across from the post office. I hadn't been in Sportsman's in months, since before the season began. The place was empty and I sat at the bar. I made conversation with Louis, the owner, whom I'd known for years—a guy who came to the island after college and never left. Occasionally, he'd show up for dinner at my place with one of his girlfriends and drive home drunk, his hand probably already between her legs

"Hey, I hear you have some weird shit happening over at your place," Louis said, in a conspiratorial whisper, though nothing on the island was secret. "Business sucks and you got all these Indians, for one thing. And a guy died?"

"Not that I know of," I said.

"That's not what I heard." Louis looked up at the planked ceiling, fingered a faded shell necklace around his neck. His face was wrinkled and a little vexed. I wondered if all of us island boys seemed alike, boyish and stunted. We were single and childless and might always be. "He died in the pool or something, right?"

Sanjiv walked in just then and put his heavy plastic bags down by the door as if they contained the most fragile flowers. He removed a thin, honey-colored wallet from his back pocket, placed it on the bar, and sat down next to me. It was unusually hot in town that day, and Sanjiv drank his beer in several gulps. He ordered another one, which he rested between his large hands, tapping the glass with his rings.

"Much better," Sanjiv said. "Now we can talk, Mr. Thierry."

"Find what you were looking for?" I asked.

"Surprisingly, yes. Completely successful." He named a few stores. "And I poked around the video shop here as well, to see what's what in a place like this. Large porno selection, one might be surprised to know."

"It can get pretty quiet around here," I said, and Louis smirked. "Long, hot winters. Long, hot summers, long hot in-betweens."

Sanjiv considered this, sipped his beer slowly, and smiled condescendingly at Louis, who got the hint and backed away. "I will have to tell Henry he is well represented. It will give him great pleasure to know that he has reached even such a place as this."

"Blaze is into porno?"

"Well, he imports it, of course. You have to these days to make any money. It is a small part of his business, in fact, but a most lucrative one. He doesn't approve of the stuff."

"Art films, he told me, epics, that sort of thing," I said. "Blockbusters. *The Eighth Moon*."

"You know that one? Ah, Henry. He's a dealmaker, an orchestrator. I am aware of all his business dealings." Sanjiv laughed. His accent was subtle and covered his words in silk. "You wouldn't think Mrs. Blaze would approve either, would you? And she doesn't, of course." He turned to face me and winked. "She pretends not to know—that and other things. It is a complicated thing, very sad, all of this, AIDS now. We have been lovers, Henry and I, for many years."

We turned back to our beers for a minute, and I felt an enormous pressure to say something, my own confession. "He wants me to help him die. He said he'd bring you here in return."

"Yes, I know that. Henry keeps a promise." Sanjiv nodded, his eyes tearing. "We're all here now to say good-bye. He doesn't look good, I agree, and I imagine he will die on this island." He took a sip of his beer. "Henry has told me about you, Mr. Thierry, that he has known you since you were a little boy, and now he will save your island for you. You're a fine businessman, a proprietor, and this is a wonderful place. You'll make a good decision about things," he said, knowingly.

"Jesus, killing a man is not a business deal," I said, angrily.

Sanjiv shook his head. "No, of course it isn't. It was never meant to be. I love him very much, and I will be sad to see him go, but sometimes this is right. You know, I will be sadder to have him dead in the end."

That evening, I was drawn to watch Sanjiv at work in the kitchen. Easily frustrated, he was also surprisingly awkward as he cooked, bending from the hips as though his back hurt him. The blade of the knife bit into his skin too often, he squinted unhappily at the chaos of chopped onions. His white shirt was stained, and the heft of the pans turned his wrists. When he rolled up his sleeves, I noticed that he wore a black bracelet like Blaze's that circled tightly against his bone.

I was not used to the thick aromas and yellow scents that rose from the pots, nor were the greengaw birds loitering around the open back door, who stopped their night singing as if another hurricane were whistling toward them. Steam pulsed from the food Sanjiv and I brought out to the dining room where Blaze, his wife, and friends were seated around several tables pushed together. They had lit a dozen candles. The few other guests watched from their tables where they were drinking and bored. The windows fogged up, and someone jumped to turn on the ceiling fan. A tape player stashed under the table hummed softly unfamiliar music.

I hadn't been invited to eat, and I had no appetite, but I saw that a place had been left at the table; they waited for me to sit down. The food was startling, and women piled it on my plate. Sweat collected under my eyes. Blaze forced small forkfuls into his mouth and chewed slowly. Every few minutes a toast would be made to him, stories of his generosity, affection, and humor. He stared at me as these testaments linked us closer together with expectation. A heavy silence fell over this farewell dinner. Some of my staff, usually long gone by that hour, smoked cigarettes on the patio and watched me. Something has happened to Kip Thierry, who sat down to eat with these lighter-dark people, they would report. I was under an island spell that had left me confused and could not be good. Nothing would ever be the same after this.

"Now we should thank our host," Blaze said, speaking for the first time that night and turning to Sanjiv.

"We appreciate your finest hospitality, Mr. Thierry." Sanjiv raised his can of Coke. "And we have made Henry the promise that we will be back next year. We will bring our families, if you will have us."

"What do you think, Sanjiv?" Blaze said. He stared at me, not unkindly. "Is a man in his position going to say no to a deal like that?"

A shadow moved behind Blaze in the darkest part of the room. My throat slammed shut, and the shadow passed behind me like a pressing heat across my shoulders. Blaze extracted something from his mouth. Sanjiv wiped his forehead and watched him with a leftward slide of his eyes. Two women whispered like rustling leaves. Cecelia's eyes darted. They were waiting for me to speak, but I couldn't. I thought I might fall over then, my head cleave like a melon on the table.

"Ah, it's all right," Blaze said sweetly, and raised a thin arm over the table. "Are you looking for someone?"

I thought he might help *me* now, when I could barely breathe. But he was talking to a little boy who had wandered into the room looking for his father and stood frozen, terrified by the sight of Blaze in the candlelight.

I was up earlier than anyone else the next morning, and wandered my island, drawn finally to the path that led to the Blazes'. At the turn of the bluff, I looked up at their cabana, which had taken a particularly hard beating in the hurricane. I'd rebuilt the pointed roof overhang myself out of aged purple heartwood, which now gleamed with its oily veins. But some angles, I realized that morning, would never be fully realigned, and hints of splinter and tarnish were visible everywhere. Up on the stone terrace, I looked into the cabana and saw the single sleeping, sheeted form of Cecelia, her blond hair fanned youthfully across the pillow. At my back, the wind had picked up slightly and blew the smell of salt and the sound of Sanjiv's liquid voice up the island.

When I looked down to the pool that eddied between the two fist-shaped rock outcroppings, even more perfectly visible from this height, the shaded light was green at that hour. The water was clear down to the sand, the slow moving parrot fish, and Sanjiv, who held Blaze in his arms like a baby just above the surface. Sanjiv said something just before he leaned down. I knew that he would drown Blaze then—and wasn't that right for these lovers?—and I would be spared. I wouldn't stop it. Sanjiv kissed Blaze on the mouth and I waited. The currents rocked them, but still Sanjiv wouldn't let Blaze go. I knew at that moment he couldn't do it; he was waiting for me.

By the time I made it down to the eddying pool, I had no idea how long Blaze had been in the water. His skin was a puckered grayish white, and he looked as bad as a person can look and still be alive. There would be no startling transformation when he died, just the relief of pain and the boredom of this. To end it now would be a mercy. Sanjiv placed Blaze, chilled and practically weightless, in my arms. Blaze didn't open his eyes, and there was no struggle as I lowered him and pulled away my hands. His body darkened the water below the surface and warmed it.

Later I watched the island police prepare to take Blaze's body away. Sanjiv had his arm around Cecelia, who told him she had felt a pinch behind her ear earlier when she was in bed. She wanted to know if he thought it had occurred at the same moment Henry died. Sanjiv said yes, it seemed they were connected that way.

Tell me what happened, an island authority said to me.

What had I seen? Two men swimming in a dangerous spot, so I'd gone to help them. I told the authority, whom I'd known since childhood, that Blaze was sick and weak. Sanjiv watched me as though I understood everything now; I had offered my island, and an act of love is no crime. So I said that Henry had drowned, and he seemed to understand the power of the currents when I showed him the exact spot where it had happened.

Hester Kaplan's short fiction has appeared in numerous publications, including *The Best American Short Stories 1998* and *The Best American Short Stories 1999*. She lives in Providence, Rhode Island.

David Walton, *Evening Out*
Leigh Allison Wilson, *From the Bottom Up*
Sandra Thompson, *Close-Ups*
Susan Neville, *The Invention of Flight*
Mary Hood, *How Far She Went*
François Camoin, *Why Men Are Afraid of Women*
Molly Giles, *Rough Translations*
Daniel Curley, *Living with Snakes*
Peter Meinke, *The Piano Tuner*
Tony Ardizzone, *The Evening News*
Salvatore La Puma, *The Boys of Bensonhurst*
Melissa Pritchard, *Spirit Seizures*
Philip F. Deaver, *Silent Retreats*
Gail Galloway Adams, *The Purchase of Order*
Carole L. Glickfeld, *Useful Gifts*
Antonya Nelson, *The Expendables*
Nancy Zafris, *The People I Know*
Debra Monroe, *The Source of Trouble*
Robert H. Abel, *Ghost Traps*
T. M. McNally, *Low Flying Aircraft*
Alfred DePew, *The Melancholy of Departure*
Dennis Hathaway, *The Consequences of Desire*
Rita Ciresi, *Mother Rocket*
Dianne Nelson, *A Brief History of Male Nudes in America*
Christopher McIlroy, *All My Relations*
Alyce Miller, *The Nature of Longing*
Carol Lee Lorenzo, *Nervous Dancer*
C. M. Mayo, *Sky Over El Nido*
Wendy Brenner, *Large Animals in Everyday Life*
Paul Rawlins, *No Lie Like Love*
Harvey Grossinger, *The Quarry*
Ha Jin, *Under the Red Flag*
Andy Plattner, *Winter Money*
Frank Soos, *Unified Field Theory*
Mary Clyde, *Survival Rates*
Hester Kaplan, *The Edge of Marriage*